Our Debt to Greece and Rome

EDITORS

GEORGE DEPUE HADZSITS, PH.D.

DAVID MOORE ROBINSON, PH.D., LL.D.

CATULLUS
AND HIS INFLUENCE

BY
KARL POMEROY HARRINGTON, A.M.

COOPER SQUARE PUBLISHERS, INC.
NEW YORK
1963

Published 1963 by Cooper Square Publishers, Inc.
59 Fourth Avenue, New York 3, N. Y.
Library of Congress Catalog Card No. 63-10267

PRINTED IN THE UNITED STATES OF AMERICA

To

MY DEAR WIFE
TO WHOM
LOVE AND BEAUTY ARE PRECIOUS

EDITORS' PREFACE

THE story of the Influence of Catullus is as fascinating as any novel. Very often that influence upon subsequent poets of later ages has been direct and immediate, but, quite as often, it is in an elusive way that the spirit of Catullus reappears in the verses of poets of other days and remote climes. It is the larger story of that direct and indirect influence that Professor Harrington has essayed to sketch in his volume for the Library " Our Debt to Greece and Rome." The Alexandrian verses of Catullus may have earned for him the epithet of the ' learned,' but it is his spontaneous lyrics that have made him immortal. The history of their influence sets very clearly before us our debt to Catullus and the value of his poetical accomplishment for the present.

CONTENTS

CATULLUS
AND HIS INFLUENCE

CATULLUS AND HIS INFLUENCE

I. CATULLUS THE MAN

THERE was no "*Who's Who*" in Rome! What would we not give for an authorized edition of such a work! If Cicero, for example, had wanted to look up quickly the personal, political and poetical standing of Catullus, he would have been as helpless as if he had been told to send a wireless to Chicago for an aëroplane to bring over a case of "Wrigley's" to the senate house! Cicero, to be sure, might have asked his fellow-orator Calvus about the latter's crony, the young Catullus from Verona, and have learned in that way many facts and no little gossip. But, alas! we cannot yet electrify into life the ashes of Calvus and listen at his lips to eloquent praise of his quondam friend. A couple of centuries later Suetonius under-took a kind of biographical dictionary of

[3]

eminent Romans who had lived in preceding generations, one department of which dealt with poets. But the paragraphs which concerned Catullus were lost to the world long ago, and the only pitiful remnants that have survived to our day consist of the dates of the birth and death of the poet as quoted by the notoriously inaccurate St. Jerome. If to these we add the reference to Catullus in Suetonius' life of the great Julius, where a reconciliation between the frank poet and the masterful Caesar is mentioned, we have all the biographical data left us by Romans living within the two centuries succeeding the death of the young Veronese. The only other fact that came out in Roman literature was the statement by Apuleius that the real name of the fair lady whom Catullus called " Lesbia " was Clodia.

It would be hard indeed to reconstruct for our imagination a poet's life out of such meager materials as the biographies of Catullus have left us, had not he himself even in his relatively small body of poetry contributed many allusions or hints that present a sort of moving picture of his career. Even so, he is far less informing about himself than was the other great Roman lyrist, Horace, whose works are full of references to himself and his achievements. How much more persistent are ideas than facts! Almost every event in the lives of the greatest men of the past is called in question from time to time by the conscientious biographer; but the theories, the feelings and the influence of such men are imperishable.

It was at Verona, the city whose name immediately suggests to us the romantic tales of which Shakespeare availed himself more than once, that Catullus was born, it matters not whether in 84 or 87 B.C.; which date is correct we shall probably never know. Verona was then a leading town of what became just about that time the Roman province of Cisalpine Gaul. The Romans had become possessed of this rich district of Italy a hundred and fifty years earlier; but only slowly was the country Romanized. It is not unlikely that there was in the Catullus family a Gallic strain to which the poet owed some of his strong likes and dislikes, as well as his sensitiveness to the beautiful in nature and in life.[1] His father was a man of some importance, a man whom the governor, Caesar, would choose as his host when passing that way. But there is little evidence of any such intimacy between father and son as existed in the case of Horace. The only other member of the family of whom we hear is a brother, apparently older, whom Catullus passionately loved, and whose untimely death in young manhood plunged the impressionable poet into a grief which was for a time quite inconsolable.

" But, brother, what with mirth was once so rife
  Is turned to sadness by thy timeless doom;
  Dead with thy death is all that cheer'd my life,
  And all our house is buried in thy tomb." [1a]

Educational opportunities in the province were but slender. The eager mind of Catullus must have made some use of what schooling was available. The poetic impulse asserted itself early. ' When first,' he writes to Allius, ' I took the pure white toga, in the days when my blooming youth was enjoying its merry springtime, I made merry enough in light verse.' [2] Probably such poems as the remonstrance addressed to Colonia,[3] the suburb of Verona, and the dialogue carried on

[6]

with the tattling house-door [4] belong to this youthful period. They certainly exhibit the intimate knowledge of the gossip of the day that we should expect to find in a young man about town, whose genial good-fellowship and ardent affections made him a favorite with all and let him promptly into the intimate secrets of loves and lovers. Perhaps such free-and-easy girls as " Aufilena " and " Ameana " belonged to the Verona society of those days. At any rate we cannot imagine Catullus as ever hesitating to express the warm affection of his youth in poetry and in all the countless other ways that young love knows so well.

We can only guess when the compelling centripetal urge of the Roman metropolis caught him away from this relatively jejune provincial existence and plunged him into the rich, full tide of life at the capital. But our guess is supported by a significant fact. In the year 62 B.C. Quintus Caecilius Metellus Celer, who had loyally supported Cicero in the preceding year in thwarting the revolutionary plans of Catiline, became proconsular governor of Cisalpine Gaul. His wife was the famous, and infamous, beauty, Clodia, sister of Cicero's bitter personal enemy, Publius Clodius Pulcher. As Clodia may be presumed to have spent at least a part of the year with her husband, and as the father of Catullus was so prominent a citizen of Verona, there is little difficulty in imagining that it was at some time during that year that the poet at his own home met this fascinating woman, who was destined to inspire, and shortly to wreck the impressionable young man's life, and that when she returned to Rome she carried his heart away with her among many similar trophies. At any rate, the next year Catullus was probably settled in Rome, which was henceforth to be counted as his real and permanent home. There is nothing to indicate that any of his family attended the young prodigal on this journey to " a far country." He was of age, and probably had already received a fair portion of his father's " goods." He never seemed to suffer quite the poverty traditional with poets and ever adhering to spendthrifts. He owned a country villa in the delightful and fashionable suburb of Tibur, as well as his charming lakeside home at Sirmio, the Sermione of today, on the Lago di Garda. No doubt he was understood to have gone to Rome for further study, and to seek his fortune. Certain it is that he soon found himself at home in the metropolitan circle of poets and other literary men, and that the fortune which he most ardently sought was fortune in love.

It was a most interesting and famous society into which he thus projected himself in the gay and exciting days when the Roman Republic was hastening on in its decline towards its fall, less than a score of years removed. At the end of September, 61 B.C., the great Pompey, who had arrived back from his successful campaign against the powerful and dangerous eastern prince Mithridates, celebrated a triumph of such magnificence that it took two days to pass in review the tokens of his victories. For the moment Pompey was the hero of the populace. We can easily imagine the fellow-countryman of Catullus, Cornelius Nepos, to whom he dedicated his book of poems,[5] and who was now about forty years of age, as having done the honors of host on this occasion in pointing out to the young Cisalpine the lions of the capital. Nepos knew everybody, and almost everything, it must have appeared to Catullus. It was he, a veritable H. G. Wells, who condensed the whole history of the world into a readable three books; and his biographies of famous men are still read by schoolboys. Perhaps, as the long line of trophies passed along, hour after hour, Nepos and Catullus stood beside some pillar in the Forum and, weary of the endless representations of cities, turned their eyes towards the notables of the day who, we may imagine, were likewise gazing at the triumph. Let us imagine the scene. In a conspicuous seat on the steps of the temple of Castor sits Crassus, the wealthiest man in Rome, whose ambitions for more wealth are unlimited, and who next year will join with Pompey and Caesar in a coalition to startle Rome and emphasize the weakness of its constitution. Caesar, explains Nepos, is just now in Spain; but great reports are coming back of his successes over there, and, as he is the idol of the democracy of Rome, there is intense expectation as to what he will do when he gets back next year. Near Crassus sits Cicero, the ex-consul, not unconscious of his own services to the state in suppressing the Catiline conspiracy a couple of years ago. But as the younger of the two Gauls studies the figure of the noted orator, he cannot for the moment think of anything but the bitter enmity that has sprung up between him and the brother of the very beauty who had enthralled his heart up in Verona, — Clodia, the reigning belle of Roman society. For Clodius had engaged in a notorious escapade a few months ago, entering in disguise a private house where a group of high-born women were celebrating the secret rites of the Good Goddess, and by his action creating a scandal of unexampled proportions, even for Rome. Clodius had bribed the jury that tried the famous case, and thus escaped conviction; but Cicero had won his eternal enmity by nonchalantly disproving the alibi claimed by the accused. Of course Catullus has heard all about it, maybe in part from Clodia herself; and the eyes of the young poet wander away to the spot where she is sitting beside her husband, Caecilius Metellus, already consul-elect for the coming year. A young dandy not twenty feet away is staring at her fascinating face; and Catullus with a start realizes that it must be the ubiquitous Marcus Caelius Rufus, who also is said to be smitten with Clodia. Nepos brings Catullus back from his musing by pointing out another of the group on the steps, Hortensius, the older rival of Cicero at the bar. He too has dabbled in poetry, says Nepos, as so many lawyers do, ambitious to leave to posterity some real literature besides their dry legal opinions. There too is Cato, the watch-dog of the Republic, grimly gazing at the pageant, but with little apparent sympathy. The young fellow over there at the left is Manlius Torquatus, who has but recently come into the politico-legal limelight by prosecuting Publius Cornelius Sulla on the charge of having engaged with Catiline in conspiracy. The charming young girl at his side is Vinia Aurunculeia, his betrothed. By the corner of the temple is another group which Nepos points out with eager interest: Gaius Sallustius Crispus, who has ambitions to write history; Titus Lucretius Carus, whose mien seems to indicate that his mind is not on the great show before him, but wandering far away in philosophic speculations; Gaius Licinius Calvus, who is good at anything in the literary line, from an oration to a lyric trifle; Helvius Cinna, who dabbles in epics; Decimus Laberius, who amuses himself with

writing mimes; and Cornificius, the critic.
With them stands also a young boy, whose
bright eyes are full of promise; but how can
Nepos foresee that Gaius Asinius Pollio will
not only become the foremost critic of Rome,
but will also, himself an author of tragedy
and history, open the first public library in
Rome? Marcus Terentius Varro, the most
learned of Roman authors, is not a member of
this company, but sits up above near Cicero.
Down in the crowd massed up to the edge of
the Sacred Street stands the young freedman,
Publilius Syrus, and beside him a Greek from
Nicaea, Parthenius by name, whose poetic
skill had set the young Roman poets all agog
to learn his art. In the same vicinity are
certain characters who would doubtless be
prominent today in our front-page journal-
ism. There is one Gellius, whose name gossip
connects unpleasantly with his step-mother
and with various other people; the young
rakes, Furius and Flavius; and some young
women whose manner is not calculated to
enhance their reputation.

But sunset is at hand and the triumph is
over. Catullus turns once again towards
Clodia; and a single meaning glance from her

fascinating eyes sets his pulse to beating violently. The crowds pour out of the Forum by various channels. It is too late to go out to his lovely home which he has just purchased on the hillsides beyond Tibur; for the road will not be safe when once darkness has fallen. So Catullus betakes himself to his bachelor apartments, Nepos accompanying him and mentioning several other literary men from Gaul whom he had not noticed in the crowd in the Forum. Why not have some of them come in with them to a little supper party at his rooms, suggests Catullus. Whereupon Nepos dispatches a slave to fetch as quickly as possible several members of the remarkable coterie of Gallico-Roman poets already in Rome, of which Catullus is destined to become the most notable member.

The group soon gathered to meet the young Veronese and enjoy his hospitality must needs include Valerius Cato, who is a leading grammarian, though sprung from Gaul, the fame of whose poems *Lydia* and *Diana* has endured; Furius Bibaculus from Cremona, who is especially endowed with a gift for biting satire; the scholarly Publius Terentius Varro, from Atax in Narbonese Gaul; Volusius from Padua, whose *Annals* Catullus later estimates as deserving no better use than that of wrapping paper for mackerel; Helvius Cinna also, from somewhere in Cisalpine Gaul, a poet so particular to bring his work to the acme of refinement that Catullus tells how he spent nine years in polishing a short account of the strange love affair of Smyrna; Caecilius from Novum Comum, who is at work on a little poem on Cybele; Quintilius Varus from Cremona, and his friend Suffenus; and the Celtiberian Egnatius, to whom Catullus at once took a violent dislike on account of his perpetual grin. The company will not be complete without Licinius Calvus, whose versatility and jovial good-fellowship would surely make him welcome in any gathering of *litterati*.

In such a rare company of choice spirits Catullus began his Bohemian life in the metropolis. His reactions to the beautiful and to the ugly were so quick and so intense that he was not long in picking from the number of men of similar poetic tastes and aspirations a few favorites and conceiving a positive aversion to others. One of the most facile of them, at first sight, was Suffenus, the friend

of Varus. He dressed elegantly, had the manners of a gentleman, and could carry on a
conversation scintillating with wit and apt
sayings. Original poetry he could reel off by
the yard, as fluently as even old Lucilius did
his satires. But the quick perception of
Catullus soon detected the flatness and stu-
pidity of the verses themselves, and it was
not many days before he sent Varus this neat
estimate of his friend:

' That chap Suffenus, Varus, whom you know so
    well,
 A charming fellow is with wit, and tales to tell;
 He writes more verses too, far more than any
    one, —
 Ten thousand of them, I presume, or more, he's
    done.
 Nor does he use, as some folks must, a palimpsest,
 But splendid paper, brand-new rolls, pink straps,
    the best
 Of parchment wrappers, ruled with lead, all
    rubbed down smooth,
 While from each end projects a' fancy boss,
    forsooth.
 But when you try to read these verses, then the
    chic
 Suffenus seems no more than any bumpkin
    freak

[16]

Or country ditcher. What a transformation that!
How can it be that any one should prove so flat,
Who but an hour ago was deemed a clever wit?
He's " farmer hayseed!" — cannot write a little
*   bit,*
When once he tackles poetry! And yet, what's
*   worse,*
He's never quite so happy as when scribbling
*   verse!*
On that he prides himself, and clearly feels his
*   oats,*
As o'er his fancied, his poetic, gifts he gloats.
But we too, doubtless, likewise fool ourselves
*   sometimes:*
Each one in turn becomes Suffenus making
*   rhymes;*
Each has his hobby, each his sad perversity;
The ugly hunch upon our back we cannot see.' [5a]

Catullus soon made the acquaintance of the
young Greek Parthenius, who was well versed
in the latest arts of Alexandrianism. For
while we can hardly believe that our young
friend from Verona had a very serious purpose to drink deep at the fountains of oratory,
philosophy, and politics, any more than had
young Marcus Cicero (though the latter was
sent to Athens, as Catullus was not, expressly

to get that type of education), he was eager
to follow up his poetic bent and to learn more
of the art from its Greek models. It was
not long before, under the tutelage of Parthenius and Valerius Cato, he knew more
metric than anybody in Rome. Nor did
he shrink from the intricacies of the Greek
mythology, after the manner of our modern
youth, who balks at the confused genealogies,
can neither spell nor pronounce the long hard
names, and is about as hazy in his general
familiarity with the tales of the classical gods,
goddesses and heroes as was poor old Trimal-
chio when he undertook to tell Homeric stories
to his well-fed guests. The apt pupil tried his
hand at various meters, new for Latin, and
practiced imitating some of the masterpieces
of Alexandrian elegy, proving himself equally
competent to reproduce the tone and manner
of a Callimachus and a Sappho.

But poets are inclined to be spasmodic in
their devotion to hard work, especially if they
are as temperamental as was Catullus. Like
the typical college "student" of our own
generation, he threw himself eagerly into
whatever made up the social life of his day,
and found a large part of his satisfaction in

the companionship of his friends. We discover indeed relatively little in his poems
about his haunts and his amusements at Rome.
He never seems to have time or inclination to
tell us much about himself, except in connection with the one most absorbing pastime of
love-making. In that connection, to be sure,
once we see him hunting for a favorite through
" the lesser Campus," the circus, the shops of
the booksellers, the temple of Jupiter, and
Pompey's Porch. But Catullus knew folks,
and delighted in boon-companions, and had
on his tongue's end all the gossip of the street
or the Forum. The violence of his affections
and of his antipathies is that of a frank,
lovable, but careless nature. Irrepressible
love and hatred bubble over from his lips.
For his enemies, or those whom he dislikes
for whatever reason, he uses the language of
the smoking-room or the frontier camp of
today. For his friends he expresses the most
ardent admiration and affection. He promptly
discovered an affinity for the brilliant young
Licinius Calvus, who was about of his own
age, and who, along with his more serious
oratorical studies, affected likewise the Alexandrian elegy. Catullus has given us a picture

of an evening spent with Calvus in amusement, by means of a match in verse-making:[6]

" How *pleasantly, Licinius, went*
  The hours which yesterday we spent,
  Engaged, as men like us befits,
  In keen encounter of our wits!
  My tablets still the records bear
  Of all the good things jotted there,
  The wit, the repartee that flew
  From you to me, from me to you;
  The gay bright verse, that seemed to shine
  More sparkling than the sparkling wine.
  And I came home, my friend, at night
  In such a fever of delight,
  With your rare wit and sayings deep,
  That I could neither eat nor sleep;
  But turn'd and toss'd and turn'd again
  With throbbing pulse and busy brain,
  Longing for dawn to set me free,
  Once more to seek your company.

  'Tis come, but here I lie half dead
  With aching limbs upon my bed;
  Whence I to you these lines have penn'd,
  Oh brilliant and amusing friend,
  That so you may divine my mood
  Of feverish disquietude!

  And now I warn you not to slight
  The love I proffer, lest, in spite,

*Dread Nemesis inflict on you
Such punishment as then were due;
A goddess she, not over tender,
So have a care how you offend her! "*

Metropolitan life, for a young man of fairly well-filled pocket-book, no fixed occupation except the pursuit of poetry, and no responsibility for the use of his time to anybody but himself, is perilous enough in any age. In some respects perhaps Catullus came off as well as could be expected, or better. If we can judge from his poems, he was not excessively interested in the pleasures of the table. Once, when a sudden illness prevented his acceptance of an invitation to dine sumptuously with Sestius, he in humorous vein attributes the attack to his foolish eagerness to enjoy such a banquet. Though other lyrists before him and after him found an important source of inspiration in the fruit of the vine, only in one brief poem does he warm to that subject. He despises avarice in others, and shows no sign of it in himself. His responsive spontaneity must have made him not merely a favorite in a large social circle, but also given him a wide acquaintance with many whose acquaintance we should have little cared to make. Perhaps city people knew each other rather more intimately when they could almost shake hands from houses on opposite sides of those narrow and crowded streets of old Rome. After making due allowance for the hyperbole of youth, we still have little sympathy for many apparently worthless characters whom the poet has pilloried to eternal disgrace. Seducers, panders, incestuous persons, old rakes like Cominius, worthless parasites such as Porcius and Socration, Asinius Marrucinus who "swiped" the napkins from his host's table, and a precious pair, father and son, who stole the clothes of men in the baths, the unspeakable Naso, bad-breathed Aemilius, poverty-stricken borrowers, hungry Aemilius, Flavius ashamed to acknowledge his mistress, and Maecilia the mistress of two lovers at once, drabs and arch villains, — it is a sorry crew of pseudo-gentilities whose masks Catullus rudely pulls off as they trip across the stage. There are doubtless those in London and New York who may thank their lucky stars that poets don't speak quite so plainly in the great cities of our own day.

But the most absorbing interest of Catullus from the moment he reached Rome was love; and the idol of his eyes and of his heart was Clodia. From the moment when he had first looked into those witching eyes which had earned for her from Cicero the epithet which Homer had attached to Juno, queen of the gods, from that moment the young poet's doom was fixed. It may have been, as has been suggested, that the fateful fascination smote through his marrow as he sat face to face with her in a boat on the Lago di Garda, entertaining thus his father's guest, before ever he saw Rome. It must have been after some such occasion, surely, that he wrote, and doubtless sent the lady, this dainty imitation of Sappho's rapturous lyric:[7]

" God, or more than God he seemeth,
 In whose eyes thy bright glance beameth,
 In whose ears thy laughter trilleth,
  Sitting near to thee;
 For that smile my senses stealeth,
 And the look that thee revealeth,
 Every word uprising killeth!
  Lesbia, love but me!
 Through my veins the hot blood boundeth,
 Fails my voice — strange murmuring soundeth —

All the world such darkness filleth,
Naught mine eyes can see."

Any fair lady might well have been flattered
by such a declaration on the part of a promising young poet. To him she was the reincar-
nation in Rome of that Lesbian damsel whose
heart was all love, and whose person was
fashioned to inspire mutual love. By him
henceforth she was never addressed through
any other name than the appropriate pseudonym " Lesbia."

For Clodia love was a game; for Catullus
it was an o'ermastering passion. To this
central passion of his life we owe the unsur-
passed love lyrics that have been the model
of all succeeding ages down to our own, and
the elusive despair of all would-be imitators.
The course of this true love, which was fore-
ordained to run with little smoothness, may
be easily traced in the poetic expressions of
the lover. He has been smitten. His fancy
runs wildly. He would be delighted even to
touch something belonging to the loved one,
to play with the pet sparrow of his ideal
beauty, the plaything of her idle moments.
The pet sparrow dies. A lament combining

most subtly a sense of personal loss with an affectionate sympathy for the lady was well calculated to win her heart. In the rehearsal to his friend Allius of his gratitude for help in forwarding their liaison we see how a meeting place was arranged where the lovers might realize the fulfilment of their mutual desires hitherto restrained by circumstances: " As at the top of a lofty mountain a bright stream leaps forth from a moss-grown rock, and gushing headlong down the steep valley crosses the midway thronged by the people, a sweet solace in his labor to the weary wayfarer when sultry heat makes the parched fields to gape; and as to mariners tossed by the black storm comes a favouring breeze with gentle breath sought by prayer now to Pollux, now to Castor: — such an aid to me was Allius; he opened a broad track across the fenced field, he gave me access to a house and its mistress, under whose roof we could together enjoy each his own love. Thither my fair goddess delicately stepped, and set the sole of her shining foot on the smooth threshold, as she pressed on her creaking sandal: even as once Laodamia came burning with love to the house of Protesilaus." [8]

Whenever it was that the idyl of *Acme and Septimius* was written, perhaps several years later, it cannot be doubted that it expresses, even if in reminiscent mood, the mutual sentiment of that golden hour of love's first complete satisfaction:

" *Septimius cried, as on his breast*
 His darling Acme he caress'd,
 ' *My Acme, if I love not thee*
 To madness, ay, distractedly,
 And with a love that well I know
 With time shall finer, wilder grow,
 In Libya may I then, my sweet,
 Or India's burning deserts, meet
 The green-eyed lion's hungry glare,
 And none be by to help me there! '
 As thus he whisper'd, Love was pleased,
 And on the right, propitious sneezed.

 Then bending gently back her head,
 With that sweet mouth, so rosy-red,
 Upon his eyes she dropped a kiss,
 Intoxicating them with bliss.
 ' *Oh Septimillus, life!* ' *cried she,*
 ' *So Love our only master be,*
 As burns in me, thine Acme true,
 A fire that thrills my marrow through,
 Intenser, mightier, more divine,
 Than any thou canst feel in thine! '

[26]

As *thus* *she* *whisper'd,* *Love* *was* *pleased,*
And *on* *the* *right,* *propitious* *sneezed.*
  And *now,* *with* *such* *fair* *omens* *blest,*
They *live* *possessing* *and* *possess'd.*
Septimius *prizes* *Acme's* *smiles*
Above *the* *East* *or* *Britain's* *Isles;*
Whilst *Acme,* *to* *Septimius* *true,*
For *him* *doth* *evermore* *renew*
Love's *first* *delights,* *and* *to* *her* *boy*
Unveils *fresh* *treasuries* *of* *joy.*
  Were *ever* *mortals* *seen* *so* *blest*
With *all* *that's* *sweetest,* *brightest,* *best!* " [9]

Clodia had perhaps never encountered anything, even in her rich experience, like the
abandon of the young poet's affection, and
had playfully inquired what limit he himself
would set to their caresses. His reply is that
of the novitiate just entering an Elysium of
love:

" *Dost* *thou,* *Lesbia,* *ask* *that* *I*
  Say *how* *many* *of* *thy* *kisses*
Would *my* *craving* *satisfy,*
  Yea, *would* *surfeit* *me* *with* *blisses?*
Count *the* *grains* *of* *sand* *besprent*
  O'er *Cyrene's* *spicy* *plain,*
'Twixt *old* *Battus'* *monument,*
  And *the* *sweltering* *Hammon's* *fane.*

Count the silent stars of night,
  That be ever watching, when
Lovers tasting stol'n delight
  Dream not of their silent ken.
When these numbers thou hast told,
  And hast kisses given as many,
Then I may, perchance, cry Hold!
  And no longer wish for any.
But, my love, there's no amount
  For a rage like mine too vast,
Which a curious fool may count,
  Or with tongue malignant blast." [10]

People began to talk, and Catullus returns to the charge with reiteration of the one idea that possessed him:

" *Let's live and love, O Lesbia mine,*
  And value at a single copper
Chatter of grey-beards too too proper!
The setting sun again will shine;
But once has set our little light
We sleep for ever one unbroken Night.
Give a thousand kisses then,
And now a hundred, and again
A thousand, and a hundred yet,
And this and that reiterate:
When these to many thousands mount,
Jumble them up — for fear we count,

Or Malice look with envious eye
On kisses mounting up so high! " [11]

As to the details of Lesbia's charms, her
lover speaks only by implication, or in superlative generalities. Somebody dared to compare
" Ameana," probably a Veronese girl, with
the Roman beauty. At this affront to his
beloved, Catullus exclaims: — ' O you lady
with neither a petite nose, nor a delicate foot,
nor black eyes, nor taper fingers, nor a clean
mouth, and with a tongue none too refined,
. . . can it be with you that folks compare my
Lesbia? What an age! How lacking in taste
and polish! ' And while acknowledging the
good points of a Roman belle named Quintia,
he emphasizes Clodia's comparative brilliancy
and indefinable superiority:

" ' *Quintia's a beauty!* ' *many cry.*
  Say fair and tall and straight of limb!
I grant each item, but deny
  Their sum is beauty's synonym.
Where is her charm? What pinch of wit
Has that large frame to season it?
  Lesbia's a beauty, all must own;
Not only wholly exquisite,
But every charm is hers alone,
And every woman's robbed of it! " [12]

Clodia's husband, Metellus Celer, was consul in the year 60 B.C.; yet even he was not too engrossed in official cares to notice the flirtation of his wife with the poet. How well Catullus understood human nature appears in an epigrammatic trifle of about this time:

"*When her husband is by, Lesbia rails at me sore;*
And he chuckles to think how she scolds me.
Thou dull ass! not to see, that her silence would more
Prove how little she thinks of, or holds me.
By these scoffs, and these flouts, I not only can find
That I long on her thoughts have been feeding;
But, what's more, that she's vext, and, to speak my whole mind,
That strong love in the storm lies a breeding." [13]

In his love-blindness it never occurs, at this stage of the game, to the somewhat inexperienced lover, that his Lesbia might play double with him as well as with a husband! True, she was a married woman; and reason should have told him that a faithless wife might well be expected to be likewise a faithless mistress. But his obsession drives reason and scruple alike from his head. In modern parlance, he believed that Lesbia and he were "soul-affinities," and no artificial ties of man-made wedlock should stand in the way of a marriage "made in Heaven!" Even after the whole turbid dream was over, and in due time the real character of Clodia was plainly revealed to him, he always thought of himself as having faithfully kept his own pledges, and could even call upon the gods in this language: — 'Ye gods, if it is yours to pity, if ye have ever come with help to souls in the last article of death, look in mercy upon me in my despair, and if I have led a life of purity, relieve me of this pernicious plague!'[14] There seems to be, in fact, something essentially Gallic about the relations of Catullus, the eager young poet, and the married woman Clodia. He cannot conceive that he is doing anything wrong. Lesbia was so splendid, and seemed herself so taken with the enthusiastic boy from the province! She too had poetic gifts and aspirations. She knew other promising young men. The attachment grew spontaneously and rapidly. But Catullus does not, like Propertius and the other erotic poets, dwell on the physical charms of his Lesbia; nor does he mention any detail of his amour that we need to expurgate from his poetry when we hand it to our wives and daughters, however untrue that may be of the abusive language he allows himself in reviling his enemies. There is nothing gross about the attachment in his mind; it is a blissful, a perfect soul-union.

When Metellus Celer died, the next year after his consulship, there were ugly hints that his wife had poisoned him. But we hear nothing of that from Catullus. He even seems to cherish for a time the hope that he may succeed the ex-consul as Clodia's legal husband. At the same time there are faint signs of suspicion on his part, that her words and her deeds are not entirely commensurate:

" *Lesbia declares she'd marry none but me,*
  Not even Jove, should he her wooer be;
  She says so: but on wind and rapid wave
  A woman's troth to her fond swain engrave." [15]

After disillusionment he refers to this stage of his infatuation thus:

[32]

" Once Lesbia vow'd she would Catullus wed,
 And scorn for him the blissful arms of Jove:
Then did my flame the lover's flame exceed;
 'Twas fond, 'twas tender as a parent's love!
I know thee now; and tho' more fierce I burn,
 Yet I thy charms more cheap, more worthless
  deem!
' How so?' thou sayst — ' 'Tis that, perfidious
  grown,
Thou'rt more seducing, but of less esteem.' " [16]

Clodia was in fact an outstanding example
of the " new woman " of her day. " Emanci-
pation " came nearer expressing a literal
truth for the sex then than that much-abused
word does in our own generation; and the
leaders in the movement, like those in the
van of many other "movements " since
Clodia's day, tended to run to extremes.
Catullus hardly needed to urge her not to
mind gossip; she already scorned it. Her
gay life, her freedom with her many friends,
in short the abandon with which she led the
most advanced " society " set of the day, were
the sources of growing scandal. She had no
intention of confining her favors to Catullus.
To him his Lesbia had been a woman *plus* a
goddess. He was rudely awakened to find

that on the other hand to her he was only one of many mere men! A new favorite, a rival, had, we hardly know when, suddenly appeared on the horizon, in the person of the young man about town, Marcus Caelius Rufus, a glimpse of whom we caught in the Forum. Caelius was eminently fitted to captivate Clodia for a time, — as long a time as she ever could be especially fond of any one man. He was a typical young blood of Roman society. He talked well, wrote well, knew everybody and every latest item of gossip about everybody. He must have been infinitely amusing to Clodia; and for a time they were a pretty pair.

Of course Caelius and Catullus had been intimate friends, belonging to the same social set; and the discovery of Clodia's new amour came as a chilling shock to the poet, and wrung from him a bitter protest:[17] 'O Rufus! whom I trusted as a friend, vainly and without cause! No! not vainly, but for a great and terrible reward. For have you not as a friend crept into my very self, alas! and, burning my poor heart through and through, stolen away from it all its happiness? Yes, yes, alas! you are the thief, the cruel poison

[34]

of my life, the baneful curse of my friendship! ' It is a reasonable presumption that
it was of Caelius, also, that he was thinking
when he penned those despairing words on
ungrateful human nature: [18]

" Oh! cease to wish from any one a kindly thought
    to merit,
  Or yet to think you can inspire a meek and
    grateful spirit;
  All are ungrateful; all, alas! kind deeds avail
    us nothing;
  Nay, more, they rather weary, cloy, and lead
    to utter loathing;
  For he in fierce and bitter hate to no sworn foe
    is second,
  Who lately had in me the one, the only friend
    he reckon'd."

Mr. Macnaghten has very happily developed the parallel between Catullus and his
Lesbia and Shakespeare and his " dark lady "
of the *Sonnets*. In each case the gifted youth
of poetic power fell under the spell of the
physical and intellectual charms of a married
woman of the nobility. In each case there
was for a time complete devotion to the flashing eye, the elegant manners and the genteel

coquetries of the fascinatress. In each case there resulted the soulful poetry of real genius. In each case the lover was for a time supplanted by a friend possessing certain superior or novel attractions for the lady. In each case the jilted one came to see that the delicate flower he believed had been stolen from him was after all but a common weed. As for Caelius, he soon found out the fickleness of Clodia's favor, and Cicero not many years later had to defend him against a charge — brought by the unconscionable lady herself — of attempting to poison his former mistress.

Catullus did not give up easily. There are plenty of poetic proofs of quarrels and at least partial reconciliations, before he finally and reluctantly determined that the liaison must be absolutely broken off, once and for all. At first remonstrances in verse evidently indicate hope of a return of the old mutual confidence, and love predominates over suspicion. Then, with added proof of Lesbia's inconstancy, the fond heart of her lover is rent asunder by the conflict of passions, and in the intensity of his heart-rending suffering he cries, with the conciseness of inimitable genius:

'I *love and I hate! You ask how I can do it?*
I *know not, but feel it: in torment I rue it.*' [19]

Finally, after fondly reminding her that his
affection had been, as he believes, unique in
its intensity and its fidelity, he reins himself
in with a violent jerk, acknowledges that the
character of the woman is past hope, and
sternly commands himself to have done with
her forever:

" 'Tis *hard to quench at once a long-nursed love;*
   'Tis *hard — but do it howsoe'er you may;*
It *is your only chance — your courage prove —*
   Easy or difficult — you must obey." [20]

Not only Caelius Rufus, but also various
other, doubtless in several cases more worthless, recipients of Clodia's favor had been from
time to time mercilessly flayed by the pen
of Catullus. As Mr. Slater phrases it, he
practiced " insult as a fine art." At any rate,
we do not waste any sympathy on the objects
of these particular attacks. The poet's portfolio was probably well-stocked also with first
drafts of poems on many subjects and in a
wide variety of styles, which had occupied
his attention when he could turn it away from

his Lesbia to his art. Meanwhile, before the total wreck of his dream of love, another great sorrow had broken into the poet's life. His brother, for whom he entertained a tender fondness worthy of so ardent a lover, suddenly died. Catullus had for a time returned to his family home in Verona, where indeed disquieting reports reached him of his Lesbia's conduct in his absence from Rome, which only served to enhance his grief over the loss of his brother. For the time being he had no taste for either love or poetry.

In due time, like the true metropolitan that he had become, he returned to his home in Rome. But the old life, as we have seen, grew more and more unbearable and impossible. When his passion had finally run the gamut from love to hatred and disgust, the opportunity to escape for a time from it all came through a year spent in Bithynia as a member of the staff of the praetor Memmius. His friend and fellow poet Cinna was also one of the party. If we are to trust Catullus himself, Memmius was not any better than the average Roman provincial governor. The year was not an ideal experience; but it served to distract the poet's mind from brooding too constantly over his recent unhappy experiences; and the new scenes, the visits to places rich in myth and legend, and the poetic associations of various kinds must have given him a new wealth of inspiration, to which we can easily trace the origin of some of his most successful poetic products. In Phrygia, for instance, was located the Attis cult, which forms the subject of one of his most remarkable and ingenious poems. And the beautiful sea pictures which adorn the *epithalamium* of Peleus and Thetis may well be reminiscences of the Aegean as Catullus himself saw it, both coming and going. Besides, though the poet, if he had any expectation of making his fortune in the rich province, was thoroughly disillusioned on that subject, he was able, probably on the return journey, to carry out a cherished desire to lay his own personal tribute on the tomb of his brother in the Troad, — an occasion which he commemorates for us in a touching little elegy: [21]

" *Brother of mine, o'er land and sea*
  At last, at last I have won to thee,
  To lay my head on thy grave and weep
  The blinding tears for thy tearless sleep,
       Brother of mine.

Brother of mine, oh unheeding dust,
That the fire has seared and the urn has crushed,
'Listen,' I cry with a fruitless faith
As I lean my lips to the ear of death,
          'Brother of mine!'

Brother of mine, who are gone from me,
Was Life so blind to the worth of thee?
I come, as our fathers bade us come,
With a last sad gift to thy lonely tomb,
          Brother of mine.

Brother of mine, to the end of time
Thy death shall live in my tear-stained rhyme.
Comrade of old, be my comrade still,
Hail yet again, and again farewell,
          Brother of mine."

It appears that Catullus had money enough
on leaving the province to buy, or have built
for him, a dainty little yacht, for the return
journey, — a craft of which he boasts not a
little when he had safely reached the shores
of his fatherland. Once it had stood as a
' whispering forest ' [22] on the heights overlook-
ing the Black Sea, whose waters first it had
taken. Then it had left astern everything
floating, whether it used sails or oars, as it
raced over the Sea of Marmora, by Thrace

and the Cyclades, and braved the stormy Adriatic. Mild [23] was the breath of spring; past were the equinoctial gales, and eagerly did the soul of the poet leap within him as he neared once more " home, sweet home." Nor did he tarry now at Verona, but hurried on to his lovely Sirmio, that 'gem of peninsulas and islands,' [24] to lay down every care and every burdensome thought, and, weary with languor from long travel, to reach his own fireside.

It was not long before the old irresistible lure of the city drew him once more to Rome. It was not now his Lesbia whom he wished to see. But there were other old friendships to be renewed. There were some new friendships and even affections. There was a new zest for the continuance of his poetic studies and achievements. Yet we can hardly think of Catullus as ever more than an intermittent student, relying on impulse rather than fixed purpose or methodical habits. Like all real poets, " born and not made," he was always tempted to write only when he felt like it. A fragment in Sapphics [25] he had perhaps penned at some introspective moment, acknowledging the tendency that he had known too well:

[41]

' Idleness, Catullus, is your misfortune:
In your idleness far too much you revel.
Idleness has ruined great kings before, and
    Prosperous cities.'

Nevertheless to this period we must assign
some of the longest and most polished of the
poems of Catullus, as, for example, the
epithalamium of Peleus and Thetis.

Roman politics were seething more than
ever now. In this field the poet had charac-
teristically strong likes and dislikes, and did
not hesitate to express them vigorously.
Cicero he compliments on being the best of
advocates. The idea that such worthless
politicians as Nonius and Vatinius should
occupy the curule chair of office he scouts as
an outrage. His admiration for the rhetorical
cleverness of his friend Calvus is reiterated in
an epigrammatic trifle: [26]

' How I laughed at a fellow in the court-room,
When just now my friend Calvus clinched the
    charges,
O, so cleverly, on the knave Vatinius!
Cried he, raising both hands in admiration,
" Great gods! look! what an eloquent little
    Tom Thumb! " '

[42]

There may have been personal reasons why Caesar and his special cronies and minions were a particular anathema to Catullus. It is not unlikely that the notorious Mamurra and perhaps others had at Verona, and possibly at Rome, cultivated intimacies that came close home to the poet. Certainly his denunciations of Mamurra are among the most violent of his abusive epigrams, and Caesar himself was not spared, when in fine contempt Catullus emphatically asserts that he does not propose to take any pains to toady to him, and doesn't even care to be informed of his good points. Caesar, however, the most patient and tactful of diplomats, found means to conciliate the fiery young aristocrat, and the rapprochement of which we have already spoken was consummated.

Among other friendships in these latter days of the short life of the poet, a strong attachment to a pretty boy, addressed repeatedly in affectionate terms under the name of Juventius, is most prominent. Even Clodia, now that Catullus had become a friend of the powerful Caesar, sent emissaries to her former lover to propose a renewal of the old tender relations. But the bluntness of the language

in which the suggestion was declined left no
longer any doubt in anybody's mind that the
love of other days was now absolutely dead: [27]

> " *Sweet, seek no more*
> *To win back my love, by thine own fault it fell;*
> *In the far corner of the field though hid,*
> *Touched by the plough at last, — the flower*
> *is dead."*

Like the flower of love, too, the life of the
poet, who was still a young man, soon faded,
drooped, and passed away. There is no evidence that Catullus was living after the year
54 B.C. Had he experienced the stormy times
of the next few years, a man of his quick
and intense sympathies would have left us
some trace thereof in his poetry. How often
it has happened that the ardent flame of
genius has all too swiftly burnt itself out!
We can hardly help wondering if Clodia, when
she heard of the death of him who had gladly
offered her all that he was or could be, took
down from her shelf a little roll, and musingly
read: [28]

> " *Was never one could say, so loved was she*
> *As, Lesbia, thou by me:*
> *Was never heart to covenant so true*
> *As mine to love of you."*

[44]

II. CATULLUS THE POET

IT has been remarked that in all ages the best lyric poetry is the product of youth, as evidenced, for example, in such shining illustrations as Sappho, Catullus and Shelley.[29] Too often, alas! the same fervency of nature that is responsible for such poetry carries the singers into social relations at which society officially shys, though when it is merely in " fatigue uniform " it condones them. Some of the loving of a Catullus, a Burns, a Byron, or a Shelley, to say nothing of poets, playwrights and actors of our own day, will not bear the critical eye of the moralist; but masterly expressions of this elemental passion appeal, as does nothing else in literature, to the human heart. In that great Roman literature which lies at the foundation of so large a part of all literature since the days of old Rome itself, Catullus was the first, so far as our knowledge goes, to utter the old deep and heartfelt note of love in the forms of lyric beauty.

But not only in this field did Catullus break the way at Rome. Whatever essays in other lyric and elegiac forms may have been made by the school of young poets to which Catullus belonged, his work only of them all has survived to us in any considerable amount. And so it is Catullus who is the pioneer, in Roman literature, not only in the personal and the formal lyric, the *epithalamium,* and the subjective and the objective elegy, but even in the epigram and the lampoon. In his short and self-indulgent life he naturally wrote no large body of verse; but we have outstanding examples of all these types in the existing collection of one hundred and sixteen poems. Nor is it likely that the poet left much other material, if any. Whoever went fondly through his portfolio after his death, and arranged his literary remains, performed this task somewhat arbitrarily, and in a rather artificial manner. Of the existing collection some poems may very likely have been published earlier; and possibly there were political squibs or personal attacks that were suppressed; though the freedom of speech in many of those which we have makes that seem improbable. The arrangement is such that the first three-score poems are the shorter lyrics in various measures, including however some that are of the epigrammatic nature; the next four are a group of longer pieces, three *epithalamia,* and the famous *Attis,* which may be said to belong, in a negative sense, to the same general line of thought; and the remaining poems, all in the elegiac distich, include longer imitations of the Alexandrian elegy, and shorter, subjective expressions of the various intense personal moods of the poet.

Besides the poems in the elegiac strophe, and the two *epithalamia* written in the dactylic hexameter, Catullus employs about ten other varieties of measure. Of these the eleven-syllabled Phalæcean, built on a trochaic basis, is his favorite mode, and in it he has composed no less than forty poems. These " hendeca-syllables " range all the way from the daintily sentimental apostrophe to Lesbia's pet sparrow, through humorous trifles like the record of the amazement of the audience at the eloquence of Calvus, down to the frank-spoken revilings of various worthless men and women who are pilloried before the scorn of the ages. Next in popularity with the poet are the Scazons, or " Lame Iambics," in which

with similar versatility he wrote eight poems.
There are three pieces in Iambic Trimeter,
and one in the Septenarius. In the Sapphic
stanza there are two samples of what Latin
was capable of producing in this ornate form.
Once he tried his hand at the greater Asclepia-
dean. Three other pieces, including a long
epithalamium, are written in one or another
combination of the musical Glyconics and
Pherecratics. And, to prove himself un-
daunted by any difficult metrical problem in
the transfusion of Greek rhythms into Latin,
Catullus has left us his amazing mastery of
the baffling Galliambics, in the unique *Attis,*
where we can hear, as it were, the jazz-like
echo of the drums and cymbals which drove
the devotees of the Great Mother in her Phryg-
ian orgies into a frenzy comparable to the
excitements of our most violent post-bellum
Terpsichorean revels. Thus through the quick
musical ear of Catullus were the melodious
rhythms of the Greeks naturalized in the
Latin tongue, and given to medieval and
modern literature.

The songs Catullus sang were mostly those
expressing the mood of the singer himself,
his admiration for a lovely lake or a hand-

some woman, his detestation of an enemy or a scoundrel, or his analysis of his own feelings in what were, or seemed to be, crises in his life. Or the subject might be a mere pleasant evening, or a humorous incident, or his appreciation of the worth of a friend or acquaintance. But he also tried his hand on some of the well-recognized themes of lyric verse which were not particularly connected with any personal experience of his own. Such was the celebration of the praises of the goddess Diana in a brief formal hymn, which paved the way for some well-known odes by Horace. This is written in a combination of Glyconics and Pherecratics which is beautifully adapted to choral singing, the rhythm of which may perhaps be imitated as follows: [30]

' In *Diana we put our trust,*
 Youths and maidens immaculate;
 Youths and maidens immaculate,
  Let us sing of Diana.

 O *great daughter of greatest Jove,*
 Child of Leto, a noble line,
 Whom thy mother on Delos bore
  Underneath the green olive,

Born *the mistress of mountains high,*
And *of woods with their verdure clad,*
And *of places remote and wild,*
        And *of rivers resounding:*

Thou *art Juno Lucina called*
By *young mothers in travail sore,*
Powerful *Trivia, Luna too,*
        Bright *with counterfeit radiance.*

Month *by month, goddess, measurest thou*
Each *year's course in the heavens above,*
Filling *homes of the harvesters*
        Full *of goodliest increase.*

Whatsoever *thy chosen name,*
Be *thou duly revered thereby;*
And, *as wonted, in days of yore,*
        Help *and save thou the Romans!* '

The *epithalamia,* again, are a new type in
Roman literature and each of the three expresses a somewhat different attitude on the
part of the poet. Moreover one of these is
really a miniature epic of Alexandrian tone,
furnishing a field for objective descriptive
writing of no small extent, and of powerful
appeal to the imagination. Similarly objective

in form appears the charming love-idyl of Acme and Septimius, whether or not we are to interpret it as actually referring to the poet's own experience. The ætiological elegy is represented by the *Lock of Berenice*. The humorous epigram is successfully illustrated in the gibe at the Roman cockney Arrius, who was so industriously engaged in murdering " the king's " Latin. And finally in the *Attis* we find a work of genius, handling with the rarest skill this difficult subject, combining subtle analysis of the emotions, brilliant description, and dramatic power, in a form of verse that would have been the despair of most of even our best masters of rhythm.

The features of the poet's manner which stand out overtopping everything else are the intensely personal character of many of his subjects and the directness and simplicity with which he expresses his mood, be it admiration, affection, grief, scorn, ridicule, or hate. As Mr. Slater has so tersely put it, Catullus is always either in " an agony or an ecstacy." His language is sometimes that of the nursery, sometimes that of the drawing-room, sometimes that of the street corners; but he wastes no words. He paints his immortal picture of

Sirmio in a few words of mere suggestion: [31]
' Sirmio, apple of the eye of all the islands
and all-but-islands which Neptune bears either
on crystal lake or ocean waste! ' The whole
inimitable story of Lesbia and her pet sparrow
is contained in ten brief lines.[32] Only three
elegiac couplets are required to express his
deepest longing for a faithful Lesbia: [33] ' O
life of mine, it is thy proposal that our love
be mutual and eternal: great gods, help her
to promise truly, from the heart and sincerely,
that we may through all our life continue this
compact of inviolable friendship unbroken! '
A few bold strokes serve to sketch for us the
ugly outlines of a Gellius, an Aufilena, or a
Cominius. Even his grief at his brother's
untimely death can be summed up in a couple
of verses, wrung from the bleeding heart of
the poet: [34]

Accipe fraterno multum manantia fletu,
   Atque in perpetuum, frater, ave atque vale.

There are really only twenty-odd, mostly
short, poems which deal directly with the love
of Catullus, if we may include three or four
others of more or less definite renunciation of
that love. There are twice as many poems

of hatred, sometimes compressed within a single couplet, sometimes extended about to the traditional " forty stripes." The diminutive of contempt plays its part in these, as the diminutive of affection does in the poems of love. But in the expressions of his contempt Catullus does not hesitate to employ also all the Billingsgate of his day. Yet he was a lovable young fellow, and true blue to his friends, to whom he addresses about fifteen of his poems. To Cornelius Nepos he dedicates his little book.[35] Veranius, just returned to his own hearthfire, his fond brothers, and his dear old mother, he welcomes [36] back as ' the best of all his three hundred thousand friends,' a common enough hyperbole, perhaps, but an engaging one on the lips of this impulsive youth. To a fellow-poet, Caecilius of Como by the beauteous lake, he sends a papyrus note,[37] complimenting him on the successful beginning of a poem on Cybele, which had already made a lovely lady madly in love with the author, and praying him to visit Verona, where he has something of importance to communicate. To a certain Camerius he describes his eager search for him among the fair damsels of the city, thus far

in vain; and there is clearly a fellow-feeling
between the two good lovers, and an eager
wish on the part of Catullus to share with
his friend the story of their loves in true
school-girl style. In a burst of grief he blurts
out to Caelius Rufus [38] his realization of the
degradation of that Lesbia who had meant so
much in turn to each of them; and he now
generously has no word of reproach for the
brilliant young dandy who had first supplanted
him in her affections, but had also himself
come to know her faithlessness. In the midst
of his poignant grief over the death of his
brother, he writes to Hortalus [39] to explain
his failure to meet adequately the request for
a light-hearted poem, and sends with his
apology the *Lock of Berenice*. Cinna's newly-
published masterpiece, the *Smyrna,* he praises
with the prophecy that its fame will travel
as far as the Satrachus.[40] In a gem of consolation he suggests to his beloved Calvus,[41] who
is in the throes of sorrow at the death of his
wife Quintilia, that if there is in the grave any
consciousness of pleasure, the lady is less
unhappy at her untimely death than happy in
the devoted love of her husband. To an unknown Cornelius he promises [42] absolute fidel-

ity in keeping a secret. To Cicero he gives
the praise of being the best of advocates.[43]
On another occasion, after his evening of poetic
extemporizing with Calvus, he pours out his
admiration for the brilliant wit of his dear
friend in superlative longing to be with him
again.[44] A most wonderful *epithalamium* [45] is
written for the wedding of his friend Manlius
with Vinia. And, when languishing with illness and despair, he begs his Cornificius to
send him a bit of the consolation that belongs
to genuine friendship.[46]

In this latter poem, and in those on his
brother's death, as well as here and there elsewhere, there are revelations of a suffering
heart, expressed with the pathos characterizing
a sensitive soul. But only occasionally do we
get such a glimpse into the riven spirit of the
man. Far oftener does Catullus prove to us
his appreciation of the humorous. There are
as many verses indicating his keen sense of
the ridiculous as there are addressed to his
numerous friends. He rallies Flavius [47] on
the mysterious mistress whose identity he
would fain conceal. Fabullus [48] he invites to
dinner, provided he bring his dinner with him.
More than once he rails at his less success-

ful professional comrades: when Calvus, as a
sly joke, sent him a poetic anthology of the
current effusions of the day, he charged
Calvus [49] in reply with trying to kill him off
on the Saturnalia, day of merry-making. To
the *Annals* of Volusius he awards [50] the palm
for being the acme of poetic badness, a mere
mass of waste paper full of countrified in-
felicities, destined to furnish ' slack tunics
for mackerel ' in the fishmarket. A trouble-
some cough resulting from a chill he laid [51]
to reading the speech of Sestius against
Antius. He breaks into rollicking laughter as
he thinks how he would love to throw [52] from
the causeway bridge into the mud below,
head over heels, the stupid dolt of a husband
in the Colonia, who has no appreciation of
the natural instincts of his sweet young wife.
A punning skit on the farm of Furius [53] states
that it is exposed to no ordinary draught from
the north or the south, but to a draft for
fifteen thousand, two hundred sesterces!
With great good humor he tells at his own
expense the story [54] of how on his return from
Bithynia he was taken by Varus to call on
his mistress, who promptly began to ply him
with questions as to his various acquisitions

during the year in the province. Catullus tried to show her that people didn't grow rich under praetors like Memmius. ' " But, anyhow," she urged, " you surely secured some fellows to carry your sedan? " ' And, thinking to put on the air of prosperity, he rejoined, ' " Of course I wasn't so bad off that I couldn't get me eight sound chaps for that! " ' But she " called his bluff," and quickly replied, ' " Pray lend them to me, for a bit! For I want to be carried right now to the temple of Serapis." " Hold on! " said I. " That was a bad break! It was my friend Cinna who got them; but what do I care? I use them just as if they were my own. But you are a stupid bore, not to let a fellow brag a little without getting caught! " ' Finally, the most amusing of all gibes at the losing struggle of an ignoramus with the aspirate [55] is that at poor old Arrius, whose refractory tongue, even when he was sailing over the Ionian waves, turned them, alas! into " Hionian " waves!

Two or three little poems reveal the intensity of his love for his homes, and especially his villa on the lovely promontory of Sirmio. Again and again he shows his delicate appreciation of the beauties of nature, usually, however, not in formal descriptions, but in incidental references, which dart forth surprisingly from the context, and in a moment set before the reader some lovely picture on sea or mountain or meadow. Often these appear in the form of similes, whose fleeting panorama is ever and anon unrolled and rolled away again by the poet. Lesbia's kisses should [56] be ' as many as the stars in silent night, looking down upon the stolen sweets of love.' The dull husband is like [57] ' an alder in a ditch hamstrung by a Ligurian axe.' The bride Vinia is [58] " like the myrtle of Asia glistening with little sprays of blooming flowerets, which the tree nymphs nurse with dew for their delight." Or she is " like the flower of the hyacinth growing in a rich man's garden." Her bridegroom " will be entwined in her embrace as the neighboring trees are entwined by the pliant vine," an everyday picture on any Italian estate. And, once more, now that the ceremonies are over, the blushing bride in her bridal chamber awaiting her loved one is " like a fair white daisy or a rosy poppy." As the three Fates chant the song of destiny for the coming son of Peleus and Thetis, they sing: [59]

[58]

" For as the husbandman, what time the grain,
Fired by the sun, is yellowing o'er the plain,
Mows the thick ears, his trenchant falchions so
Shall smite the sons of Troy, and lay them low."

When Lesbia came to him at the trysting
place, his friend Manlius, who arranged the
meeting, was like the

" hill-born brook, which, afar off silvery
        gleaming,
O'er his moss-grown crags leaps with a tumble
        adown;
Brook which awhile headlong o'er steep and valley
        descending,
Crosses anon wide ways populous, hastes to the
        street;
Cheerer in heats o' the sun to the wanderer
        heavily fuming,
Under a drought, when fields swelter agape to
        the sky." 60

And the crown of all the tropical achievement
of Roman poesy are the two wonderful similes
put in the mouths of the maidens and the
youths respectively in their poetic emulation,
in the second noble *epithalamium* of Catullus: 61

MAIDENS

" As *in a garden grows some floweret fair,*
Safe from the flocks, safe from the ploughman's
share,
Nursed by the sun, by gentle breezes fanned,
Fed by the showers, admired on every hand,
There as it coyly blossoms in the shade,
Desired by many a youth, by many a maid;
But pluck its flower, its witchery is o'er,
And neither youth nor maid desires it more.
So is the virgin prized, endeared as much,
Whilst yet unsullied by a lover's touch;
But if she lose her chaste and virgin flower,
Her beauty's bloom is blighted in an hour:
To youths no more, no more to maidens dear.
Oh Hymen Hymenaeus, be thou near! "

YOUTHS

" As *grows a widow'd vine in open fields,*
It hangs its head, no mellow clusters yields;
So droops the fragile stem, its topmost shoot
With nerveless tendril hangs about its root;
That vine no husbandman nor rustic swain
Hath cared to tend or cultivate or train;
But if by happier chance that selfsame vine
Around a husband elm its tendrils twine,
Then many a husbandman and rustic swain
Its shoots will tend and cultivate and train.

[60]

Even such the virgin, and unprized as much,
That fades, untended by a lover's touch,
But when, in fulness of her maiden's pride,
Some fitting mate has won her for his bride,
She's loved as never she was loved before,
And parents bless her, and are stern no more."

The *Peleus and Thetis* is full of marvellous pictures of sea and land, of the blue expanse of ocean, the pellucid waters peopled with nymphs, gods and goddesses, the flecks of foam, the long swell of the waves, the pine groves of Pelion, the flowers on the Thessalian plains, and the festal holiday on the farm, when raking, pruning, and plowing are interrupted and ' the necks of the bullocks grow tender.' Moreover, the poet's mastery of metaphor turns his language constantly throughout his poems into one mold after another, producing an endless succession of pictures for the reader, — the cobwebs in the purse of Catullus, the ' pig of an Umbrian,' the ' feather-footed divinities,' the ' shining tresses ' of the marriage torches, the ' flashing eyes ' of the sun's ' golden face,' the ' whirling tide of love,' a very ' Harpocrates ' of silence, the merry laughter of the waters of his ' Lydian ' lake, or the dark road along which t sparrow started for the "country from bourne no traveler returns."

Such was the art of Catullus, conditioned by his pulsing humanity, his sensitiveness to sound and color, his wide-ranging imagination, his delicate appreciation of humor, his fidelity to friendship, his open contempt for shams and rascals, his frank and often ultra-blunt language, and his downright sincerity,— all this in the whirl of the most up-to-date society in the Roman capital, where he was caught in all the newest and most impetuous currents of the literary and social life of the last years of the Roman Republic. Sometimes he is a word-painter because he is trying his hand on the tricks of the Alexandrians, sometimes because he is visualizing for us his own experiences. Sometimes he is a metrical experimentalist, vying with his fellow-poets. Love is a consuming fire in his soul, and the grossest wrongs done to that love are wonderfully slow to cool the passion of his faithful heart. But love is not, in his case, analyzed and described in long-drawn-out raptures; a few burning lines speak the truth, and admit us to a share in his gladness or his distress. The vials of his wrath are opened suddenly and terribly, from time to time. Then he does not hesitate to utter the language of opprobrium in a way that would put a newly-returned " doughboy " to shame. But if Catullus lapses at times into expressions of coarseness or obscenity, it is never for its own sake. He does not, like too many epigrammatists of succeeding generations, create these biting lines for the fun of it, or to pander to a prurient fashion; he speaks his mind because, in his judgment, reason, no less than passion, compels him to such utterance.

The diction [62] of the poet has, accordingly, a generous colloquial content, and a considerable group of words which belong essentially to prose. For a poet who delved so deeply into Greek sources, he has no very extensive list of Greek derivatives. Diminutives, many of them of his own invention, he employed freely to express a wide variety of shades of meaning, from tender affection to contempt. There are nearly half a hundred nouns of this class, and some thirty adjectives, to say nothing of experiments in the same line on verbs and proper names. Epithets of all sorts abound, and particularly noticeable are a score of those picturesque compounds which

[63]

poets frequently love to fashion, made to order by Catullus, — like ' wave-sounding,' ' forest-roving,' ' feather-footed,' and ' woods-loving.' The intensity of the man is amply emphasized by merely observing the formidable list of his compound verbs. In his adverbs there is the greatest variety of form. Inasmuch as " father " Ennius was the last great Roman poet before his own times, it is not strange that a few archaistic tendencies appear in his diction as well as in his treatment of the dactylic hexameter. His study of Alexandrian models doubtless encouraged these tendencies, so far as the hexameter is concerned. But Catullus is an Alexandrian only on occasion, when, so to speak, on dress parade. We like him better in his simple manner of everyday life.

The *Peleus and Thetis* gives us an inkling of what Catullus might have produced in the maturity which was denied him, or which, perhaps we ought to say, he denied himself. Like one of his most brilliant successors, Propertius, who after a fitful dream of passionate life, was apparently just settling down to achieve new types of Latin poetry, so Catullus may very possibly have been trying his hand on epic models even when came the moment for that hand to be stilled forever. The lack of unity in this longest of his poems, together with the various interesting parallels [63] between it and passages in the great didactic work of his contemporary genius Lucretius, has called forth the suggestion that Catullus, who was a friend of the same Memmius to whom the *De Rerum Natura* was dedicated, had had a chance to read the latter before he wrote at least parts of the *Peleus and Thetis*. Perhaps he had read parts of the work of Lucretius before it appeared as a whole; but its publication took place only a short time before the death of Catullus. It is not impossible then that the episode of Ariadne, for whom it has been suggested that Lesbia was the real model, — although it may well have been that the poet was also quite familiar with the now famous statue of the sleeping Ariadne, — was about the last thing that Catullus wrote. If so, he was producing proof of his dramatic genius and of his descriptive imagination, gifts which might well have led him in later years to more elaborate works of a genuine epic character.

Such was the literary heritage which Catul-

lus left to posterity. " It is in short lyrics
of personal passion or emotion that the genius
of Catullus is most unique; but the same high
qualities appear in the few specimens he has
left of more elaborate lyrical architecture.
. . . The *epithalamium* . . . has in its clear
ringing music what is for this period an almost
unique premonition of the new world that rose
out of the darkness of the Middle Ages . . .
not again till the Florentine art of the fifteenth century was the picture drawn with so
true and tender a hand." It is our pleasant
task to see what the literary heritage of
Catullus has meant for the world in the two
succeeding millennia, up to the present day.

III. CATULLUS IN THE ROMAN EMPIRE

THE complex influences that shape civilization are inextricably intertwined. In a beautiful tapestry we could perhaps unravel a thread of gold traversing the pattern; but to account for the tapestry we must also consider the discoverer of the tapestry idea, the inventor of the machinery that produces it, the caravans of camels slowly bringing the raw materials from the east to the western world, the evolution of the road system of Europe under the Romans, the growth of wealth, the demands of royal courts, the modern expansion of trade, methods of distribution, and many other more or less relevant topics. If we would know the elements which Catullus has contributed to our modern life and culture, we must trace various streams of expanding influence exerted by his work from his own day to ours in Rome, continental Europe, and England. We owe unbounded gratitude to the unknown compatriot of the poet, who in the early years of the fourteenth century rescued from oblivion a single mouldering manuscript of his works, that each of us may today enjoy his own copy of these poems. Were that all, we might, even so, assert for Catullus an important influence on our own culture of life and letters, as a model for our taste in poetry and music, and as an interpreter of the life and ideals of that great age which forms so important a part of the foundations of all modern civilization. After long medieval neglect Catullus has certainly come into his own in our day. Professor Mackail, representing Oxford ideals of poetry, groups [64] Sappho, Catullus, and Shelley as a unique trio of singers. Professor Sellar [65] esteems Catullus as the only rival of Sappho among ancient poets of love. Professor Munro [66] judges thus: " To match the perennial charm of the Catullian lyric we must abandon the soil of Latium and betake ourselves to Alcaeus or Sappho, ay and join with him or her the Muse of Archilochus as well; or else jump over the ages and come at once to Burns and Goethe." But we cannot be content to consider merely the present-day popularity of our author. It is a familiar truism that " in the classics we have the great

original of almost all modern literature." [67]
And so, before we turn to the translation,
quotation and imitation of Catullus in more
modern times, and to the inspiration derived
from reading him given to our own literary
products, we must follow out the several lines
of influence exerted by his poetry from his
own day for the next millennium and a half.

Other Roman writers attacked larger
themes, completed more elaborate and extensive works of literary art, or polished more
carefully their literary jewels; but no Roman
showed greater genius and versatility or gave
a greater impetus to different schools of poetry
than did Catullus. With him, in the great
Roman tradition which has been the world's
model ever since, practically began genuine
lyric poetry, the erotic and the ætiological
elegy, the *epithalamium* and the epigram;
and also from his epyllion influences and in-
spirations reached out to the great epic poets
that were to come.

In the classical period of Roman literature
but one other notable lyric poet was produced.
Horace went much further than Catullus in
adapting the Greek lyric meters to Latin, and
he lived long enough in his comfortable position

as Augustan poet-laureate to polish leisurely
into perfection of form a very much larger
body of lyrics than his predecessor ever undertook; but Catullus had pointed the way, and
even in the perennial success and universal
popularity of Horace, we must recognize to
some extent the influence of Catullus on all
succeeding literature. Horace, to be sure, is
not very generous in giving credit to his prede-
cessors, especially his own countrymen, for
such suggestion and inspiration as he derived
from them. Nor is there any very long list
of conscious imitations which we can detect.
Horace took his own advice pretty consist-
ently, and only after severe criticism and much
re-writing, and not until the original forms
were lost or concealed, did his poems reach
the public. But who will deny that Catullus'
Hymn to Diana was the only Latin model that
he could study for the elaboration of his own
Secular Hymn or of his *Ode* in honor of Leto
and her divine children? And when Horace
sings of the sincere lover,

" *Whether in Afric's burning sands he rides,*
 Or frosty Caucasus' bleak mountain-sides,
 Or wanders lonely, where Hydaspes glides,
  That storied river," [68]

[70]

he is probably thinking of Catullus' Septimius, who swears

> "*a love that well I know*
> *With time shall fonder, wilder grow*"

with this oath,

> "*In Libya may I then, my sweet,*
> *Or India's burning deserts meet*
> *The green-eyed lion's hungry glare,*
> *And none be by to help me there.*" [69]

In Horace's ode it is a wolf which he playfully pictures as more fearsome than a lion:

> "*For as I strayed along the Sabine wood,*
> *Singing my Lalage in careless mood,*
> *Lo, all at once a wolf before me stood,*
>   *Then turned and fled:*
> *Creature so huge did warlike Daunia ne'er*
> *Engender in her forest's wildest lair,*
> *Not Juba's land, parched nurse of lions, e'er*
>   *Such monster bred!*"

In the matter of Horace's famous *curiosa felicitas* also it has been well noted by Professor Mendell [70] that in this ode the *sive — sive* phrase is borrowed from one [71] of the

two Sapphic odes of Catullus, and the *dulce
ridentem* from the other; [72] while the *otium —
otium* of the one-stanza Sapphic fragment of
Catullus is imbedded in Horace's sixteenth
ode of the second book. Various striking
imitations on the part of Horace are cited
by Noël, such as the Horatian *flagrantia
detorquet ad oscula cervicem;* [73] his *tunc nec
mens mihi nec color Certa sede manet;* [74] the
lascivis hederis ambitiosior idea; [75] and others.
And as for the passionate emulation of Acme
and Septimius to surpass each other in their
vows of devotion it is hardly possible to help
feeling with Mr. Munro [76] that Horace's neat
little dialogue with Lydia [77] was the result of
meditation on the part of the Augustan poet
upon the *Acme and Septimius* of the Republican lyrist. We cannot forget that the earlier
poet showed the later one what could be done
with Greek measures in Latin, and left him
immortal examples of the lyric of love, of
friendship, of religious adoration, and of that
lampoon which Horace in his earlier career
so bitterly employed against the objects of his
hatred. Even in the use of the poetic epis-
tolary form Catullus antedated Horace, we
must remember, even though the Augustan

[72]

poet made in his *Satires* a slighting remark about his Republican predecessor.[78]

The later Roman lyrists, if any are really worthy of the name, while imitating, if rather feebly, the metrical forms left them by Catullus and Horace, are artificial and offer little of the lightness and grace of a Catullus. When Statius is describing a banquet to which he was invited with his " Lord God the Emperor," or enlarging upon the merits of the newly-repaired Appian Way, or dwelling on the details of the magnificence of a friend's country villa, there is no place for the spontaneous lyric of personal feeling. The sending of the lock to Aesculapius,[79] however, recalls the *Lock of Berenice*. When, moreover, he remonstrates with Grypus for sending him a worthless book for a holiday present, we can readily catch in his description [80] of the book he had himself sent Grypus, " as gay as purple and new parchment and a pair of bosses could make it," [81] a reminiscence of Catullus' praises of the form of the poetaster Suffenus' pretty book, while the worthlessness of the contents of the one .book is a reminiscence of the similar contents of the other volume. And in the hexameters, celebrating the virtues of Melior's dead parrot,[82] the poet tries by a wealth of rhetorical embellishment to make up for the lack of genuine feeling which Catullus had voiced in his little gem of a poem on the death of Lesbia's pet sparrow: " Shrill rang the portals at the pecking of thy beak. Alas, today the doors speak their own vexation. Tenantless is that blissful prison; vanished the scolding voice that filled the princely mansion! . . . Mourn, mourn, ye birds together! Bear your dead companion to the funeral fire; and, one and all, learn ye this new dirge: ' The parrot, — the glory and the pride of the fowls of the air, the radiant ruler of the east, is dead, is dead! ' "[83] How ponderous this seems by comparison with the simple lament of Catullus: ' Mourn, all ye Loves and Cupids, and ye men of finer feeling. The sparrow of my lady is dead, her sparrow, my lady's darling, which she loved more than her own eyes! ' Even in poetic commonplaces, as on the shortness of life, expressed, for example, in the latter part of the *Consolation* on the death of Glaucias,[84] — " Day and night pass away, — aye, and the stars also, nor is the solid earth saved by her massy fabric," — we can hardly fail to recall

Catullus, crooning to his Lesbia: ' Suns may set and rise again. But when once the sun of our brief day has set, we must forever sleep the night that knows no waking.'

Ausonius, the learned professor of Gaul, down in the fourth century, quotes Catullus' dedication of his volume, referring to him as the " poet of Verona." And when, in one of his little poems,[85] he exclaims: ' Let us live, wife, as we have, and let us keep the pet names which we assumed when bride and groom! Let no day bring us change as we grow older, but may I ever be to you a youth, and you to me a girl,' our thought flashes back again to Catullus.[86] Scholars [87] have detected numerous other signs that Ausonius knew his Catullus either at first or second hand, like the striking farewell to Acilius Glabrio,[88] phrased in almost the same language used by Catullus in his tender farewell to his brother, or, for example, the onomatopoetic verse,[89]

Icta pedum, tentis reboant cava tympana tergis,

borrowed, presumably, from a verse in the *Attis,* which closes with the phrase, *ubi tympana reboant.*[90]

[75]

Apollinaris Sidonius, the noble Gaul who as politician and ecclesiastic in the fifth century saw the end of the Western Roman Empire and the beginning of the Dark Ages of barbarism, was evidently well acquainted with earlier Roman literature, including Catullus; but, while deeply learned and highly endowed with literary gifts, he was too engrossed with monarchs and prelates and the official life in which he basked to come down to the simplicity of a lyric style of half a millennium earlier, although he tried his hand with some success at various Latin lyric forms that were invented in those remoter days.

But if Catullus and Horace were too perfect to be much more than the despair of those in the later Roman Empire who aspired to eminence in the field of the lyric, their popularity and influence were evidently very wide in various other fields. Of Catullus in particular the vogue was such that his influence went far to shape the forms and ideals of most of the kinds of poetry chiefly affected at Rome for the next century. It is not strange, though the most perfect specimens of his art were not composed in the elegiac distich, that the relatively large number of

his collected poems which are in that measure
— nearly one half — should have early
grouped him with the elegists. Even up to
modern times the popular grouping of the
Roman elegists consisted of Catullus, Tibullus, Propertius, and Ovid; and from the beginning of printed editions of classical texts, the
house of Aldus and other great publishing
firms were wont to print Catullus, Tibullus,
and Propertius together. Propertius himself
mentions Catullus as one of his chief prede-
cessors in elegy, ' through whose elegies
Lesbia has become more famous than Helen
herself! ' There are abundant parallels in
Tibullus, — the haste to enjoy love while
youth lasts, the joy of stretching one's limbs
on the familiar bed, the frankness of love's
revelation, the bride coming to the groom,
and various pictures of the wedding time, the
hanging of garlands on the door of the loved
one, the good old simple days before men
sailed the treacherous seas, the holiday for
the beasts of burden.[91] Every now and then
Propertian expressions flash before us the
memory of some immortal poem of Catullus,
like ' Love sneezing a fortunate omen,' or
the ' spider spinning her web over the shrine.'

Lygdamus, the mysterious poet of the Tibullus circle, recognizes Catullus as 'the learned
poet,' who 'told in verse the story of faithless Theseus.' When Ovid penned his tenderly beautiful elegy on the death of Tibullus,
he expresses his belief that if there is any
after-life at all, Catullus and his friend Calvus will welcome the shade of Tibullus at the
gate of Elysium. In Ovid's own poetry there
is plenty of imitation of Catullus. He was the
first to try to match the matchless little poem
on the death of the pet sparrow, producing,
to be sure, a brilliant elegy on the death of
his Corinna's parrot, but in his elaboration of
the theme missing the directness of appeal to
the reader's heart which Catullus made so
naïvely. Repeatedly, not only in the elegiac
poems, but also in the *Metamorphoses,* does
Ovid show how close a student he was of his
illustrious predecessor. For example, four
times in as many different poems he treats
somewhat at length the story of Ariadne. And
there is an imitation of the description of
Catullus' yacht in Ovid's description of his
journey to his place of banishment. Sulpicia
too, the one woman poet of the golden age of
Roman Literature, in the brevity, frankness,

and fervor of her little elegies of personal passion can hardly have had any other model than Catullus.

But what of Virgil, the supreme epic poet of the Romans, who was the idol of patriotic Augustans, who stood in the place of an inspired sage to the Middle Ages, and who has been the source from whom is drawn so much inspiration for epic and other modern poetry? As has been well shown,[92] Virgil apparently had an early " Catullian period in his career," when he was a special student of the two great Republican poets just before· him, Lucretius and Catullus. In the *Ciris*, for example, the influence of Catullus is palpable. Some of the *Catalects* are obvious parodies on Catullian poems, the most clever of which is that on the Sabine muleteer (after the *Yacht* of Catullus), who 'claims to have been the fastest of all muleteers, and that never a racing taxi could pass him, whether one had to go to Mantua or to Brescia.' In the famous fourth *Eclogue* also, where Virgil optimistically foresees a new Golden Age, his thoughts and expressions hark back to the *Peleus and Thetis* of Catullus, as he describes the blessings of the new day and makes the *Parcae* give the command to their spindles: ' Hasten on, such ages! ' Moreover, in *Aeneid* there are numerous proofs of Virgil's intimate acquaintance with Catullus, where he has borrowed sometimes the form, and again the tenderness, of his inspired original. Striking verbal parallels, for example, are:

Carbasus obscurata dicet ferrugine Hibera (Cat., 64.227), and

pictus acu chlamydem et ferrugine clarus Hibera (*Aen.*, 9.582);

Quae Syrtis, quae Scylla rapax, quae vasta Charybdis (Cat., 64.156), and

Quid Syrtes, aut Scylla mihi, quid vasta Charybdis (*Aen.*, 7.302);

Invita, o regina, tuo de vertice cessi (Cat., 66.39), and

Invitus, regina, tuo de litore cessi (*Aen.*, 6.460);

and various others; while passages in the *Aeneid* where the thought came from Catullus are represented by the description of Dido's palace (after that where Peleus and Thetis were wed), the simile of the fading of the purple flower cut down by the plow as descriptive of the death of Euryalus (after that of Catullus' slighted love), the even more

elaborate simile in the lament for Pallas
(after that of the perfect flower of maiden-
hood, as described by the chorus of girls in
Catullus' second *Epithalamium*), and perhaps
the familiar one of 'the aged ash upon the
mountain top, quivering, tottering, and fall-
ing,' as did Troy on its fatal night. More
than this, it is the Ariadne of Catullus who
becomes the inspiration for, and ultimately
develops into, the Dido of Virgil; and nowhere more clearly than in this tragic figure
of the disappointed and abandoned queen do
we see how much of his characteristic sense
of "pity," of "tears for things," Virgil owed
to the tender-hearted Catullus:

" *Down dropped the fillet from her golden hair,*
  Dropped the light vest that veiled her bosom fair,
  The filmy cincture dropped, that strove to bind
  Her orbèd breasts, which would not be confined:
  And as they fell around her feet of snow,
  The salt waves caught and flung them to and
    fro," — [92a]

a picture of the desolate Ariadne, standing
amid the seaweed, sure to touch the sympathetic imagination of later epic poets, sculptors,
and painters.

Also in the annalistic epic of Silius Italicus appear signs of the free use of Catullus, *e.g.* in the borrowing of the figure of the tresses of flame. The same figure is used also by Seneca, Manilius, and Valerius Flaccus, while Persius copies the moral that we cannot see our own faults any more than we can see the burden on our own backs.

But it is in still another field of literature that we find our poet even more closely and constantly followed, and most copiously imitated, namely, the epigram. Hardly any other title is more potentially inclusive than that of epigram. It may be humorous; it may be biting; it may be apothegmatic. In any case it must be short, and have some point, real or apparent.

" The qualities rare in a bee that we meet
  In an epigram never should fail;
  The body should always be little and sweet,
  And a sting should be left in the tail."

In the days of Catullus the connotations of the term " epigram " were less definitely determined, even, than now. Yet how far many of his spicy little verses fulfilled its conditions the Romans were not slow to observe; and as wit, often a rather caustic wit, was always popular at Rome, and the lampoon a favorite weapon of personal attack, or of general satire, Catullus became the preferred model in this line for the whole Roman world.

Amazingly popular it was for even the most dignified and genteel of Romans to dabble in epigrammatic and other light poetry, often merely as an amusement. Indeed when, as was too often the case in those times, it took what from the standpoint of our day was an indefensibly risqué tone, it was gravely defended by serious worthies like Pliny on the same hardly tenable ground that Catullus had taken in excusing such poetry: 'A good poet, must be himself pure; his verses need not be, provided they be graceful and witty.' Pliny sets down as a praiseworthy accomplishment the ability to match Catullus or Calvus in that style of verse.[93] The same lame defense is repeated, often enough, as the centuries pass; we find it echoed, *e.g.* in an epigram of Ausonius: [94]

> "*Lais and Thais, neither name*
> *Of very specially good fame,*
> *My wife reads in my song:*

" ' 'Tis nothing but his way to jest,
He makes pretence,' she doth protest,
' He could not do me wrong.' "

Even women might write such poetry, — as
has not been their custom in more modern
times, — like the younger Sulpicia, at the end
of the first century, who sang to her lover, or
husband, Calenus, such songs as would becloud
the reputation of a similar poetess today.
Yet we need not tarry to be too harsh in our
judgment of this literary phenomenon in such
an age. Phases of human depravity vary with
epochs. There are unspeakable things in
Roman literature; but we can hardly guess
what Pliny or Sulpicia, acquainted though they
were with Latin comedies and pantomimes,
would have said about the front page of any
metropolitan journal of today, or what they
would have thought of a modern sex-problem
novel by one of our leading female novelists.

Martial, the greatest and most justly famous
of all the ancient epigrammatists, echoes the
same Catullian defense, in these words accord-
ing to an old version:

" Let not these harmless sports your censure taste!
My lines are wanton, but my life is chaste,"

[84]

which remind us of the close of Herrick's *Hesperides:*

" Jocund his Muse was, but his life was chaste."

This, however, is but an incident in the complete devotion of Martial to his acknowledged model and ideal, Catullus. As the influence of Martial is widespread and commanding throughout all European epigrammatic literature, it is important for our study to see how much he owed to Catullus. Nearly a score of times he mentions Catullus by name, adding various epithets. Sometimes it is the traditional " learned " Catullus, a phrase used thrice already by Ovid. Again it is " elegant Catullus," or " tender Catullus," or " tuneful Catullus." The esteem in which Martial holds him crops out in all sorts of connections: " tones even two Catulluses could not match;" [95] " but may I be to you less than Catullus alone;" [96] " he brings your time some honor, and is not far behind Marsus and elegant Catullus;" [97] " so belike tender Catullus ventured to send his *Sparrow* to great Maro; " [98] " as much Verona owes to her Catullus, as small Mantua owes to her Virgil." [99] These couplings of the names of Virgil and Catullus remind us that Ovid, in writing the epilogue to his *Amores*, expresses the prophetic hope that he shall be famous as the pride of his Pælignian country, as Mantua is famous for her Virgil and Verona for her Catullus, thus singling out these two as in his mind the most noteworthy names of Roman poets before his own day.

At least a half dozen times Martial refers to those favorite poems of Catullus on Lesbia's sparrow, as for example: " If you shall have such a bird as Lesbia, beloved of Catullus, mourned, here it can dwell; " [100] " Issa is naughtier than Catullus' sparrow; " [101] " her plaything and her darling, not such a one as Lesbia, the mistress of tender Catullus, deplored, when she was forlorn of her sparrow's roguish tricks;" [102] " my Stella's ' Dove,' that ' pretty pet ' (I must say it, though Verona hear me!), has surpassed, Maximus, the ' Sparrow ' of Catullus. So much is my Stella greater than your Catullus as a dove is greater than a sparrow." [103] Referring to the poem on Lesbia's kisses, he begs, — " Give me kisses now, and by Catullus' measure; if they be as many as he said, I will give thee a Sparrow

of Catullus;" [104] and again, — " Rome gives
you as many kisses, when after fifteen years
you have just returned, as Lesbia never gave
Catullus." [105]   And in imitation of Catullus,
reckoning up the number of kisses desired, he
writes: [106]

" O *Diadumene! come, kiss, and kiss me more
    and more;*
    *How oft?   As well say count the waves that
    ocean fill,*
  *The myriad shells that scatter'd lie on the Aegean
    shore,*
  *And bees that wander o'er Hymettus' flowery
    hill,*
 *Or in the crowded theater the cheers or hands
    that wave*
    When all the people see a-sudden Caesar come;
 *I will not have what sweet Catullus ask'd and
    Lesbia gave:*
    *Few are the joys he craves who number can
    the sum.*"

Martial realized how far Catullus was beyond him in power to handle difficult metrical
problems, and himself undertook no great
variety of measures. For this he defends himself in these words: [107] " Because I do not
pride myself on topsy-turvy verses, nor read

backwards in obscene Sotadics, because nowhere does a Greekling echo answer you, nor
does graceful Attis dictate to me Galliambics,
. . . I am not, Classicus, a bad poet after
all;" and in this defense he pays a very genuine compliment to Catullus for one of his
most remarkable achievements, the *Attis*.

We may not linger to cite the numerous
imitations of Catullus by Martial, sometimes
in phrase, sometimes in subject matter, sometimes in the abusive or allusive language of
the two poets. It is already clear enough how
thoroughly Catullus was the master and
Martial the pupil. The importance of this
fact in the case of an epigrammatist who was
such a favorite as was Martial throughout the
whole succeeding history of Rome, and whose
imitators have ever since been legion, can
hardly be over-estimated. Nor should we
forget that Augurinus claims Catullus and
Calvus as his models for similar verse.

Catullus was indeed often cited, or mentioned, or referred to by the writers of prose
and verse from his own time down to the end
of the Empire, — by Varro, Seneca, Velleius,
Quintilian, Tacitus, Suetonius, Gellius, by

learned commentators and grammarians, and even by Christian writers.[108] The eminent critic Quintilian, about a century after the poet, compliments him on the success with which he had handled the lampoon, calls his little satire on Arrius a 'noble' epigram, and refers to others of his poems, including the *epithalamia*. After another century the grammarian and anecdotist Gellius quotes Catullus in various connections, and tells an interesting story of a dinner party at which among other guests was a Spanish rhetorician, who, after being entertained by some songs of Anacreon, was told that the Romans had not anything of that style to show except a few poems of Catullus and Calvus.

We must pause just long enough to call attention to one special type of poetry which, after Catullus had in masterly fashion shown how to deal with it, languished long, apparently for want of courageous imitators. This is the *epithalamium*. The two genuine wedding songs of Catullus, and the epyllion of *Peleus and Thetis*, written in diverse forms, and abounding in beautiful description, striking imagery, and delicate feeling, might well cause those to hesitate who would emulate

these qualities. Not before Statius does another example occur in Roman literature. In
his *epithalamium* on the marriage of Stella
and Violentilla, the following reminiscence of
Catullus' on the wedding of Manlius and
Vinia occurs: [109]

" *When Nature, with mysterious hand, shall mould*
  The tiny features of thine infant face,
 May we thy father's beauty then behold,
  And more than all thy mother's matchless
    grace."

Again, after the lapse of centuries, Claudian
in his *epithalamia* recalls Catullus: [110]

" *Then Cytherea bears away*
 The weeping maid, whose pleading arms
 Cling to her modest mother's breast,
 And well, I ween, her looks attest
 The ripeness of her charms."

And yet again: [111]

" *Venus chose the Muse's son*
  O'er nuptial rites to reign supreme,
 And but for him no bridal bed
 Is blest; no brandished torches shed
  Their hymeneal gleam."

[90]

And in Claudian's *Rape of Proserpina* we find this passage, recalling the lament of Ariadne in the 64th of Catullus: [112]

> " My daughter, torch like this for thee I never
>   hoped to bear,
> And yet my wish was but the wish of mothers
>   everywhere,
> A happy bridal for my child, glad flambeaux
>   flaring high,
> A joyous hymeneal sung beneath the open sky;
> Thus 'mong the gods shall Lachesis without
>   distinction rave,
> And the dread name of deity be impotent to
>   save."

We have thus seen the influence of Catullus all through succeeding Roman literature. He was constantly admired, quoted, imitated. His *Sparrow* song was the father of a lineage of poems on pets running down through Ovid, Martial, Statius, and their successors. He gave inspiration to the main lines of lyric, epic, elegiac, epigrammatic, epithalamic poetry, and to the ruling *vers de société*. These great streams of poetry have never ceased flowing, to our own day, but have rather spread into innumerable outlets, ever bringing beauty and

[91]

inspiration into many fields of thought and literature. We cannot in this little volume trace all those streams. Other authors in this series discuss our debt to Ovid, Horace, Virgil, and Martial respectively. But, as we leave them for the present, we must not forget that their debt, in turn, to Catullus was very great. In passing we may also remark that in important respects these eminent poets never ›measured up to their original. To quote a foremost English critic of Horace,[113] — " In power of sarcastic expression, he is inferior to Catullus," whose " lampoons are perhaps the most powerful expression of concentrated scorn in any language." " Horace nowhere reaches such heights of creative imagination as Catullus reaches in the *Attis,* nor is he capable of the sustained union of vivid feeling with vivid imagery which we find in the *epithalamium* in honor of Manlius and Vinia." And Mr. Cranstoun, the elegant translator of many Latin poets, expresses thus his estimate of Catullus: [114] " *Attis* has no rival in any language. The *Peleus and Thetis,* again, has passages of far higher epic sublimity than any other Roman poem. Virgil has not attained the grandeur of the Ariadne, in the famous episode of Dido, nor the tender pathos of the parting of Aegeus and Theseus, in the interview between Aeneas and his sire on the downfall of Ilium."

Our present task, however, is to consider more specifically the direct transmission of the influence of Catullus to our own times.

IV. CATULLUS IN THE MIDDLE
AGES AND THE RENAISSANCE

AFTER the end of the Western Empire, the streams of the Catullus influence would seem to have run for a time in rather deep and narrow channels. Indications point towards the existence of only a very limited number of Catullus manuscripts, as the Empire waned. The Christian poet, Paulinus of Nola, in the fifth century, shows but slight knowledge of him. The *epithalamium* of Paulinus himself is more scriptural than classical. In Africa, where for a time Latin literature had a vigorous, if somewhat exotic, growth, the Christian didactic poet Dracontius, towards the end of the fifth century, in some minor poems not essentially Christian in character, shows more familiarity with Catullus than the chance references in many other writers of this later time which merely betray what may be but second-hand knowledge of the poet.[115]   Corip-

pus, too, another African poet, of the sixth
century, seems to have known something of
Catullus. Yet it does not appear that Lux-
orius, and the other contributors to the so-
called *Latin Anthology,* drew anything whatever direct from Catullian sources. Numerous quotations, on the other hand, have been
detected in Latin inscriptions, to show that
some of the most apt expressions of the poet
lingered in the popular phraseology, and were
incorporated in Christian, as well as pagan,
epitaphs and other epigraphic memorials.
Otherwise Catullus for several centuries seems
to have practically disappeared from sight
and knowledge, except for an occasional, often
rather unintelligent, reference. The grammarians and glossarians now and then quote
a word or a phrase. Isidore, the seventh
century Spanish bishop, tries to quote him
once or twice, but confuses him with Cinna.
In the ninth century the German monk Wala-
frid Strabo groups Verona and her Catullus,
Mantua and her Virgil, Greece and her
Homer, and Corduba with her Senecas,
quaintly, awarding thus by implication an
eminence to Catullus that sheds an illuminat-
ing ray into the literary darkness of this

epoch. A copy of a poetic anthology made in the same century, and now in Paris, contains the *epithalamium* which is No. 62 in the Catullus collection. When Bishop Rather of Verona in a sermon delivered there in the year 965 spoke apologetically of reading the pagan authors Catullus and Plautus, he probably referred to the only known manuscript of Catullus at that time, preserved from destruction in some way in the birthplace of the poet, perhaps one of the two hundred and eighteen manuscripts presented in the ninth century by archdeacon Pacificus to the canons of Verona.[116] Notker of St. Gall in the eleventh century had heard of him.[117] William of Malmesbury, the English monk and historian, in the twelfth century has scanty traces of his poems; and Hieremias de Montagnone of Padua, in the thirteenth century, makes a few brief citations in a collection of moral sentiments. Albertino Mussato,[118] the dramatist, at the beginning of the fourteenth century, shows traces of a knowledge of Catullus; and a collection of Latin poems was passed around between him and other men of letters in which there are references to his poetry. Thus in the darkness which preceded the European dawn of the Renaissance had almost all knowledge of the poet vanished.

But in the early years of the fourteenth century a manuscript of Catullus reappeared at Verona, whether it was the one read by Bishop Rather or some other one, — the discovery, at any rate, being ascribed to an obscure Veronese compatriot. Petrarch early made the acquaintance of this manuscript treasure, in his eagerness to know the great works of ancient classical literature; and before it disappeared again permanently, some time during the next century, the important copies had been made which, now located severally in Oxford, Paris, and Rome, are the chief foundations of our present text of the writings of the poet. So, in Italy first, some first-hand acquaintance with Catullus again began to be diffused. Pastrengo, Boccaccio, and Salutati evidence a certain familiarity with his poems. Petrarch himself had a manuscript containing various classical writings, in which are a number of citations from our author. Here and there in the Latin writings of Petrarch are references to Catullus; but more important and interesting is the evident influence which the old Latin poet had upon these Italian productions. Not only does the self-analysis of Catullus in his passion, so full of contradictions, for Lesbia find many an echo and many an elaboration in the sonnets of Petrarch addressed to his unapproachable Laura, but also several other passages can be quoted which seem to have their inspiration in Catullus. Catullus tersely remarks that 'what a woman says to an ardent lover should be written on the winds and the rushing waters.' [119]   Petrarch expands this futility thus:

> "*Happy in visions and content to pine,*
> *Shadows to clasp, to chase the summer gale,*
> *On shoreless and unfathom'd sea to sail,*
> *To build on sand, and in the air design.*" [120]

Catullus would have as many of Lesbia's kisses 'as the stars which in the silence of the night look down upon the stolen sweets of human love.' [121]   The Italian poet, after dallying at length with the concept of the starry heavens by night, when, for love of Laura, he has no rest, at length exclaims: [122]

> "*Oh! might I be with her when sinks the sun,*
> *No other eyes upon us but the stars.*"

Petrarch's verse,

" Amor, che m'ha legato, e tien me in croce,"

recalls the experience of Catullus with Juventius.[123]   If the inspiration from Catullus was present in the lyrics of " the first modern man," as Petrarch has been concisely described, it would be difficult to estimate how much Catullus has through him meant to the European scholars and litterateurs who derive their new life from the Revival of Learning, which Petrarch did so much to promote.

It would be rash to assert even a belief that Dante knew or used Catullus. Yet it is not an impossibility that he saw the Verona manuscript or a copy of it. At any rate there is a striking parallel between the Catullian emphasis on the unique beauty of his Lesbia [124] and the enthusiasm of Dante over a lady who slighted him:

" For blest in her are met
  A perfect body and a mind as fair,
  Save that some grains of pity wanting are." [125]

And as Catullus confesses himself unable either to cease to love or any longer to wish her well, so Dante, confused by his passion, cries out: [126]

" So charm'd am I with the bewitching light
Of the false traitor's eyes, that have me slain,
That I return again and yet again
To meet new death and fresh-envenom'd slight."

The two great Italian poets of the six-teenth century culled choice flowers from the garden of Catullus. It may have been due to direct borrowing, or through the medium of Virgil's imitation,[127] that Ariosto in the *Orlando Furioso* images the death of Dardi-nello in the form which Catullus had used for the passing of his passion for Lesbia: [128]

" And cold and pale the body sunk in death:
Like some fair flower, whose vivid lustre fades,
If chance the ploughman's share its stalk
  invades."

Certainly there can be no question that Ariosto draws from the second *epithalamium* [129] of Catullus the elaborate simile in which Sacri-pant in the unknown presence of his Angelica describes his ideal maiden: [130]

" The spotless maid is like the blooming rose
Which on its native stem unsully'd grows;

Where fencing walls the garden-space surround,
Nor swains nor browsing cattle tread the ground:
. . . .
The earth and streams their mutual tribute lend,
Soft breathe the gales, the pearly dews descend:
Fair youths and amorous maidens with delight
Enjoy the grateful scent, and bless the sight.
But if some hand the tender stalk invades,
Lost is its beauty, and its colour fades:
No more the care of Heaven, or garden's boast,
And all its praise with youths and maidens lost.
So when a virgin grants the precious prize
More choice than beauty, dearer than her eyes,
To some lov'd swain; the power she once
*   possess'd,*
She forfeits soon in every other breast:
Since he alone can justly love the maid,
To whom so bounteous she her love display'd."

The pagan hosts are described as count-less,[131] in the language of Catullus announcing his desire for unnumbered kisses of Lesbia.[132] He who can enumerate them, can

" count the stars, when Heaven with all its eyes
At midnight hour the lover's theft descries."

Other Catullian passages which may be men-tioned as having been apparently used by

Ariosto are: Ariadne's protest that henceforth no woman should trust the vows of any man, the picture of the dawn upon the sea,[133] and the snub offered to the lady whose charms cannot compare with those of Lesbia! [134]

Tasso, likewise, captivated by Catullus' simile [135] illustrating the beauty of virginity, resorts in his *Jerusalem Delivered* to the curious device of putting the same moralizing strain into the song of a bird in the garden of the palace of Armida: [136]

" Behold how lovely blooms the vernal rose,
  When scarce the leaves her early bud disclose;
  When, half inwrapt, and half to view reveal'd,
  She gives new pleasure from her charms conceal'd.
  But when she shows her bosom wide display'd,
  How soon her sweets exhale, her beauties fade!
  No more she seems the flower so lately lov'd,
  By virgins cherish'd, and by youths approv'd! "

To Ariosto and Tasso, be it remembered, all modern literatures are heavily indebted.

In the *Triumph of Cupid* Petrarch represented himself, after gazing on a company of celebrated lovers and poets including Virgil,

Catullus, and Sappho, as being led away to the home of Venus, where

> "*all the while, dreaming of liberty,*
> My *soul, made light and quick by great desire,*
> I *comforted by looking on past things.*" [137]

Such was indeed the spirit, for a time, of the Renaissance, to feed on the newly-discovered treasures of the classical literatures, and from them gain inspiration for the future. No sooner are the poems of Catullus again accessible than we find them eagerly studied and sedulously imitated by those who belonged to the new world of letters. Guarinus of Verona, who went to Constantinople to learn Greek, was proud of his townsman Catullus, and quotes him enthusiastically. Antonio Beccatelli, in his poem *Hermaphroditus,* begs his friend Galeaz to find him a copy of Catullus.[138] 'I am eager, my dear Galeaz, to find Catullus, the better to humor my lady. The merry girl prefers to keep reading these tender poets all the time, and prefers thy measures, learned Catullus. Only the other day she teased me for him, supposing no doubt that her favorite singer was among my books. " I haven't his little volume," said I, " light of my life, my nymph. But I will get one; you may expect a copy." She insists, begs, and threatens. So, by all the gods, my dear fellow, — and may Cytherea grant you every wish! — I beg and beseech you, hunt me up that booklet, that I may regain favor with my goddess.'

The famous scholars Pietro Bembo and Marullus wrote Latin verse in imitation of Catullus, Marullus in particular addressing a hexameter production to the lake Benacus on which had been situated the darling of the poet's heart, his villa at Sirmio. Publius Faustus Andrelinus in his *Bucolics* imitates Catullus here and there. Giovanni Pontano (1426–1503), addressing *Fannia,* combines various ideas from Catullus: " Girl, more beautiful than a soft rose, which the spring winds bring forth and which the Mother of dark Memnon waters with dew in a garden, . . . then the short glory of the flower dies and the tired petals droop; the blossom falls from the naked stem and its short honor perishes. . . . Then let us enjoy the sweet and flowering spring of youth and its short-lived flower." Andrea Navagero (1483–1529), on his return from an embassy in Spain, seems to imitate Catullus' greeting to Sirmio: "After these many toils of mind and soul I see you again, and make joyful offering that through your favor I may drive care from my heart." In the same poet's *Inscription for a Fountain* he is apparently thinking of the Catullian simile which compares the aid given him by his friend Allius to a mountain stream reaching the parched plains and the travellers' highway. Marc Antonio Flaminio (1498–1550) writes *To the Muse of Sirmio:* "O Muse, who cherish the comely white shore of Sirmio and teach the sacred grove of olives to murmur of beautiful Lesbia — we dedicate to you an altar of green turf and then bowls of honey and bubbling milk. . . . Come then, O white maiden, and speak your songs to me, so that Hyella may be immortal even as your most lovely Lesbia." [139]

Meanwhile, soon after the invention of the art of printing, one of the first of the *incunabula* was the *Editio Princeps* of Catullus, Tibullus, Propertius, and the *Silvae* of Statius, printed probably in 1472 at Venice, possibly a year or two earlier. This epoch-making edition of Catullus was followed by a number of editions by the most famous scholars dur-

ing the next hundred years, notably by Parthenius in 1486, Palladius in 1492, Alexander
Guarinus in 1521, Muretus in 1554, Achilles
Statius in 1566, and Joseph Justus Scaliger in
1577. In the north of Europe Isaac Voss was
in the seventeenth century the first of the dis-
tinguished line of scholars and editors who in
Holland, Germany, and France have chosen
the works of Catullus as the field in which
to display an erudition as vast as it has been
almost incredible. Niklaas Heinsius also left
notes on Catullus. In France Passerat and
others carried on a similar tradition.

The scholars and poets of these Renaissance
centuries in which Latin is the language of
learning and of polite letters show many a
trace of the influence of Catullus. In the
mass of Latin verse left by Julius Caesar
Scaliger is a section of short poems dedicated
to the *Manes* of Catullus, written, many of
them, in the favorite Phalæceans of Catullus,
and evincing a thorough acquaintance with
the language, manner of expression, and lines
of thought of his master. He calls him in the
opening dedication the 'greatest, best, and
most learned poet, whether the Muse inspires
him to sing in sweet whispers in the fields of

Elysium, or the silvery waves of Sirmio try
to rival him as he sings.' The little poems
abound in Catullian quips and turns of expression, in the characteristic diction, and in
the sort of subject familiar to Catullus. Some
are addressed to Cupid, some to various fair
women; some deal with Calvus, some with pup-
pies or thrushes; and some are quite Catullian
epigrams. In an independent poem on the
Lacus Benacus he employs the Glyconics and
Pherecratics of Catullus, and as he progresses
in his apostrophe to the poet's lovely lake
waxes eloquent: ' Thou art a match for the
hallowed waters of Helicon's mount; nay, but
thou dost far excel them, fuller than a fountain of gold. Who is, or shall be, or ever has
been able to rival the sound of thy liquid
throat? Yet thine offspring was the pure vein
of Catullian poesy.' The famous *Basia* of
the Dutch Johannes Secundus are quite Catullian in character. In the German Latin poet,
Petrus Lotichius Secundus, in the sixteenth
century, we find phrases or whole lines quoted
from Catullus. Tobias Scultetus, of the same
group of poets, sings, in genuine imitation of
Catullus' *Sparrow,* of the turtle-dove of his
Sophy:

' *Turtle-dovelet, daily mourning with so gentle
       voice your fate,*
 *With your pretty bill soft cooing, as from Sophy's
       hand you ate,*
 *While for me you sought her favor in the hours
       that now are flown,*
 *Let your sorrow be forgotten and remember but
       mine own.*'

How far the new enthusiasm over Catullus
aroused by the discovery of the famous manuscript in the fourteenth century traveled during Petrarch's own generation it would surely
be rash to assert.   Mr. Snell [140] thinks: " that
Petrarch's influence did not extend to the
Welsh mountains may be taken for granted."
But why, if the Welsh Petrarch, Dafydd ab
Gwilym, knew his Homer and his Virgil,
Horace, and Ovid, may it not well be that
the new Catullus inspiration too had per-
meated even to those rugged hills?   Surely
we think at once of the *Sparrow* of Catullus
on reading in Dafydd: [141]

> " Go, *thou Blackbird,*
>   To *the proud and slender maid,*
>   And *unto her show*
>   How *much for her I grieve;*

[108]

And *thou, Thrush,*
Singing on beautiful branches,
Take all my plaint
To the brilliant fair."

In England, the direct influence of Catullus is traceable at least as early as the beginning of the sixteenth century. But the consideration of English literature must be deferred for the moment and given a chapter of its own.

In the Romance literatures, the influence of the Renaissance becomes important in the early part of the sixteenth century. The forms developed by Petrarch appear even in the Spanish-Italian Chariteo,[142] about the end of the fifteenth century, while the source of the thought can be followed back to Catullus and other classical writers. In France the lyric poetry of the sixteenth century was ushered in by a definite imitation of the classics and a school of writers who undertook to improve the character of their national literature by an intimate study of the models of Roman literature and an importation of their diction. Clement Marot [143] was the first great French poet to commit himself definitely

to this manner. Ovid and Martial, to be sure,
were the Roman classical poets whom he
chose especially to follow. But Catullian
influence is not lacking. In his epigram on
Queen Eleanor's pet dog [144] he weaves together phrases belonging originally to both
Martial's poem and its original, the *Sparrow*
of Catullus. In that addressed to Jan [145] we
go back through Martial's *Non amo te, Sabidi,*
to the original *Odi et amo* of Catullus:

> " Jan, je ne t'aime point, beau sire,
>   Et ne scay quell' monde me poind,
>   Ne pourquoy c'est; je ne puis dire
>   Sinon que je ne t'aime point."

And here and there, where the imitation is
less definite, there is a suggestion of a Catullian origin.[146] With Ronsard and the rest of
the lyrists of the so-called " Pleiade " an even
more definite influence of Catullus is mani-
fest. Ronsard repeatedly refers to Catullus,
coupling his name usually with those of the
other Roman elegists, or their successors. So
in the *Élégie à Cassandre*:

> " Mais que me sert d'avoir tant leu Tibulle,
>   Properce, Ovide et le docte Catulle,
>   Avoir tant veu Petrarque et tant note,". . .

In the *Élégie à son Livre* the models of his style are thus revealed:

" Dy luy que les amours ne se souspirent pas
  D' un vers hautement grave ains d' un beau stile
      bas,
  Populaire et plaisant, ains qu'a fait Tibulle,
  L'ingenieux Ovide, et le docte Catulle."

It is, of course, in the elegies of Catullus in particular that this tradition of the *doctus poeta* is justified; and in the *Amours, Chanson 1*, the epithet disappears, and there seems to linger a reminiscence of Lesbia's countless kisses. The same reminiscence appears again in an ode *À Cassandre,* which begins:

    " Ma petite colombelle,
    Ma mignonne toute belle,
    Mon petit oeil, baisez-moy,"

and, after an imitation of the *Basia* of Johannes Secundus,[147] returns to Catullus thus:

    " J'en demanderay plus qu' onques
    Tout le ciel d'estoiles n'ent,
    Plus que d'arene poussée
    Aux bords, quand l'eau courroussée
    Contre les rives s'esment." [148]

Ronsard puts Cynthia, Propertius, Catullus, and Tibullus in the later group of *Amours*. In *Gayete II*, with Catullus and Tibullus is joined Marullus; and in the *Discours Contre Fortune* it is Muretus:

> " Dwin Muret, tu nous liras Catulle."

When Ronsard sings:

> " A*h take these lips away; no more,*
> N*o more such kisses give to me,*
> M*y spirit faints for joy,"*

we can hardly fail to recall the rapturous verses of Catullus:[149]

> lingua sed torpet, tenuis sub artus
> flamma demanat, sonitu suopte
> tintinant aures, gemina teguntur
> lumina nocte

and recognize the influence of their spirit upon the age of Ronsard. The relation of Ronsard to his models has been neatly phrased by Andrew Lang in his *Letters to Dead Authors:* " Methinks thou hast . . . been glad that the old notes were ringing again and the old French lyric measures tripping to thine ancient harmonies, echoing and replying to the Muses

of Horace and Catullus." Another enthusiastic imitator of Catullus and other Latin
poets was Mellin de Saint-Gelais, a leading
representative of the Renaissance in France,
who imported the madrigal from Italy, and
was the first to compose original French sonnets, although Marot had used the sonnet
form before him, in translations.

Joachim du Bellay, a protagonist of the
movement to enrich the French language and
literature from classical sources, wrote in both
French and Latin. He advised the study of
such classical models as Ovid, Propertius,
Tibullus, and Catullus, for the " amplification "
of French, and even urged his countrymen to
" adopt also into the ' famille Francoyse '
those tripping hendecasyllables as of a Catullus or a Pontanus." In Latin elegy he named
his beloved Faustine " Columba," and the
reminiscences and imitations of Catullus are
manifold. When, after she has been for a
time lost to him, he at length regains her, he
joyously breaks forth: [150]

' Now restored to me is my dear Columba;

  .   .   .   .

More than my very eyes I loved my darling,
And her kisses and pretty prattling murmur,

[113]

Merry ways, and sweet little saucy follies,
Far outvied all the eager ardent billings
Of Catullus' famous little sparrow.
For she was honey-sweet, a shining beauty,
Handsome, fair-complexioned and most entranc-
ing,
More entrancing than all of your honied
beauties.'

Perhaps most interesting of all these Renaissance French poets in his treatment of Catullus is Antoine de Baïf. His favorite method was to paraphrase his originals, choosing certain details which he would amplify, and sometimes combining two originals in one paraphrase. Starting, for example, with the *Lugete, o Veneres Cupidinesque* of Catullus he builds thus on his theme: [151]

> " Sus larmoyez Amourettes,
>   O Mignardises tendrettes,
>   Sus larmoyez tendrement.
>   Le passereau de m'amie:
>   Le pauvret n'est plus en vie,
>   Le pauvret qu'elle aymoit mieux
>   Que la clarté de ses yeux."

On the basis of Catullus' *Vivamus, mea Lesbia* he writes: [152]

" Vivons, Mignarde, vivons
        Et suivons
    Les ébats, qu'Amour nous donne.
Sans que, des vieux rechignez
        Renfrognez,
    Le sot babil nous estonne."

Partly from this same original, and partly
from the *Quaeris, quot mihi basiationes* he
weaves the following: [153]

" Ma vie, mon coeur, mon ame,
    Mon miel, ma rose, mon bâme,
    Tost mon cou soit enlassé,

    .   .   .   .   .

Mille baissers ie demande
    Et mille et mille, friande."

And the theme of the Catullian *Surripui tibi,
dum ludis,* he varies from this beginning: [154]

" Comme d'un pousse scavant,
    O douce esperance mienne."

Baïf has imitations also of the eighth, fourteenth and twenty-third poems of Catullus.

The spirit of Jacques Tahureau was such
that his contemporaries compared him with
Catullus. This spirit breathes in such lines as:

*" And where is the rich sea whose coral vies
With her red lips, that cannot kiss enough? "* [155]

We can hardly within the narrow limits of
this little book discuss in detail either the
personality or the product of the many trans-
lators and imitators of Catullus who now
sprang up in the France and the Germany of
the Renaissance. Certain poems were special
favorites; indeed throughout the centuries it is
remarkable how small was the circle of poems
that were considered most representative of
Catullus, and, as such, were outstanding bea-
con lights in the history of literature. The
third was imitated by Henri Estienne and by
Passerat; the fourth, by Sixte Octavien,
Estienne, by the famous scholar Lipsius, in
the form of an apotheosis of a pet dog, by
Martin Braschius, and by Valens Acidalius,
the latter using it for a parody on the theme
of a red rose.

Paul Schede, the German poet who wrote
under the pseudonym of " Melissus," wrote
parodies on Nos. 8, 15, 26, 27, 38, 46, 48, 51
(in Alcaics), 53, and probably others. He it
was who at Heidelberg, the first important
German center of humanism, translated Marot

for the Germans, and gave an important impetus to the German Renaissance epoch, which really begins in the seventeenth century. Leading representatives of this movement in Germany were the lyric poets Weckherlin and Opitz. The ever-recurring Catullian theme of lovers' kisses without number appears, for example, in Weckherlin's twenty-eighth poem:

" ' für dich hab ich mehr qual und müh,
   dan man kan körnlein sands alhie
   und tropfen in dem meere finden.'
   Myrta gab ihm hierauf antwort!
   ' o meinen seelen süsser hort,
   ich trag zu dir in meinem herzen
   mehr lieb dan augenblick im jahr;
   mehr, dan stern hat der himmel klar,
   leid ich für dich liebreiche schmerzen.' " [156]

And yet again, in the *epithalamium* on the marriage of Filander and Gloris,[157] we discover the same motif:

" Mehr dan stern in der klaren nacht,
   mehr dan blümlein des frühlings pracht,
   mehr dan auf Hybla binen fliegen," etc.

Weckherlin has given us also an imitation of the Catullian comparison between Quintia and his Lesbia: [158]

[117]

" Die Lylla sei schön, wie mit fleiss
    vil rühmen, kan nicht gestehen:
    sie ist (ohn witz) lang, aufrecht, weiss,
    recht wie ein hübsches bild zu sehen.
    Da meine Myrta schön, süss, weiss
    und ganz holdselig zu bekennen,
    verdienend aller herzen preis,
    die schönheit selbs allein zu nennen."

It was Martin Opitz who adopted, and persuaded his countrymen for the time-being to adopt the poetic principles and ideals of humanism as formulated by Ronsard, although he himself was more successful with the theory of poetry than with its practice. All sorts of classical themes and types appear in his various styles of poetry. Occasionally here too we find what may be only an indirect reminiscence of Catullus,[159] in such a passage as this:

" Ach, Liebte, lass uns eilen,
    Wir haben Zeit,
  Es schadet das Verveilen
    Uns beiderseit.

   .   .   .   .   .   .

Drum lass uns jetzt geniessen
    Der Jugend Frucht,

Eh' als wir folgen müssen
Der Jahre Flucht."

But we cannot follow as widely as we
would, either in Italy, France or Germany,
or in the remoter rings of the ever-widening
circle, the influence of Catullus on European
Renaissance poetry and literary ideals. And
there is much that is intangible, which prop-
erly belongs to our subject. We have seen
that both in Latin poetry and in that of the
vernacular the inspiration given by Catullus
is evident in the lyric, elegiac, epigrammatic,
and other forms which were handed down by
the Roman tradition to the medieval Latin
and to the modern languages; that the themes,
the pictures and the spirit of the many-sided
genius of Catullus proved immortal as the
Renaissance of learning and literature awakened Europe from her long stupor; that even
the most characteristic things about the Catullian diction, his wealth of diminutives and
descriptive compounds, were eagerly taken up
and imitated systematically in the new classical school of poetry in France and Germany.
But one should read widely in the poetry of the
Middle Ages to realize how the Sapphics and

elegiacs, knowledge of which came from Catullus, were the leading vehicle of all the poets' thoughts. Moreover the debt of the whole mass of popular Latin medieval lyrics, sacred or profane, to these ancient lyric models of poetic form is incalculable. These countless varieties of accentual and rhymed verse traveled far afield from the quantitative classical orthodox forms. But who shall estimate the influence of the dainty rhythms and the ardent spirit of Catullus [160] in the ultimate fruitage of student songs in such forms, for example, as these? —

> " Tempus adest floridum,
> surgunt namque flores,
> vernales mox in omnibus
> iam mutantur mores." [161]

> " Si tenerem quam capio
> in nemore sub folio,
> oscularer cum gaudio.
> Dulcis amor! " [162]

> " Iuvenes amoriferi,
> virgines amplexamini!
> Ludos incitat
> avium concentus.

> O vireat, o floreat, o gaudeat
> in tempore iuventus!
>
> .   .   .   .
>
> Tua pulchra facies
> *me fey planser* milies,
> pectus habens glacies,
> *a remender*
> statim vivus fierem
> *per un baser.*" [163]

And when Mr. Symonds renders into English one of these invitations to mutual love:

> " *Try, my girl, O try what bliss*
> *Young men render when they kiss!*
> *Youth is always sturdy, straight;*
> *Old age totters in its gait.*
> *These delights of love we bring*
> *Have the suppleness of spring,*" [164]

we recognize the old spirit of the young Catullus renewed in the medieval springtime.

How much did the new metrical structure which was raised in Italy and France and copied all over Europe, with its sonnet, canzonet, madrigal, and all those refinements of metrical form, owe to this medieval accentual poetry? and how much, in the ultimate analysis, to Catullus? And how much all modern literature owes, directly or indirectly, to his immortal enthusiasm and his sensuous appreciation of all that is lovely in nature and in human love because so perfectly manifested in the verses of the young Roman poet of two thousand years ago! We cannot in this little book cover the whole field of research into these complex questions. They are broadly suggestive; the answers must likewise be more suggestive than comprehensive. We must hasten to note briefly how the awakened enthusiasm over Catullus spread over Europe in the study and translation of his works, and then must pass on to consider somewhat more in detail the influence of the poet upon English literature.

V. CATULLUS ON THE CONTINENT SINCE THE RENAISSANCE

THE awakening of classical scholarship all over Europe gave rise to various learned editions of Catullus in different countries. In the seventeenth century the French savant Passerat wrote his commentary, and the Dutch scholar Isaac Voss prepared an edition full of recondite learning. The German Doering and the Italian Conradino in the eighteenth century continued the succession. In the nineteenth century the great wave of classical scholarship in Germany brought the critical editions of Lachmann and Baehrens, and the various studies by Ribbeck, Haupt, and Schwabe, as well as popular or school editions like that of Riese. The abundant periodical literature at the end of this century was crowded with discussions on Catullus. Doctors' theses about Catullus multiplied. At the beginning of the twentieth century the suggestive commentary of Friedrich caused in his learned contemporaries astonishment at its comprehensive appreciation. This classical learning

[123]

impressed the form and the romantic spirit of
Catullus upon the educated world, and left
innumerable traces on the literature of all the
European countries. Already in the *Miscel-
lanies* of Barlaeus (1646) we discover this
superlative appreciation of Catullus' lyric
eminence: ' Were it imaginable that Jove
should sing the story·of his amours, he would
expect to speak with this tongue, none other '
[i.e. the speech of Catullus]. Stephen Pas-
chasius expresses the popularity of Catullus
and Dionysius Cato (an odd pair of favorites!), by saying that though one may find
many imitators of Cato and Catullus, ' nobody
could for one brief hour attain the heights of
Cato's moralizing or the tenderness of the
verse of Catullus:'

> " At nullus Cato, nullus et Catullus;
> Nullus qui potis horula vel una
> Durum moribus assequi Catonem,
> Mollem versibus assequi Catullum."

Imitators enough there were indeed. Translations of the whole of the Catullus collection
were made into French by the Abbé de
Marolle in 1653, by Pezay in the eighteenth
century, and by Eugene Rostand in the nine-

teenth century, and into German by an anonymous translator in 1790, and by Heyse in the
middle of the nineteenth century. The popu-
larizing of Catullus was further promoted by
many versions of individual poems. In Italy,
Alamanni, Nerucci, Torelli and Ippolito Pin-
demonte of Verona (1753–1828); in Germany,
Mayr, Gurlitt and Ramler; in France, poets,
too numerous to catalogue, amused themselves
with turning into the vernacular such Catullian gems as especially appealed to their individual fancy. Noël in his Paris edition of
1803 sheds a flood of light on the popularity
of Catullus, — and we must not forget the
influence of the French literature of this
period on that of England. The *Peleus and
Thetis* is a favorite for translation; versions
in their respective languages by Le Gendre,
Eisen-Schmidt and Severio Broglio d'Ajano
are worthy of mention. Of the first *Sparrow*
poem, — besides various French imitations
and translations, one on a canary, — the German Conradinus produced a Latin version,
beginning:

" Turtur, deliciae meae nigelle,
    Qui mi saepius excutis molestas
    Tristi e pectore cogitationes," etc.

Of the second *Sparrow* poem we may note
several imitations, one by the Italian Georgius
Anselinus Nepos, expressing the grief of a
father at the death of his daughter; one, by
Andre Naugeri, a Venetian, on the death of
a pet dog; another by Conradinus the German; another by Hadrianus Marius the Bel-
gian; besides a Greek version by Monnoye
and a Latin re-translation of the same by
Nicholas Bourbon; and others by various
French writers. That by Corrozet begins:

> " Pleurez, joyeuses amourettes,
> Pleurez, caresses joliettes,
> Pleurez, tous hommes de plaisir
> Puisque mort a osé raisir;"

the one by Durand, thus:

> " Sus! plorons le passereau
> Que gist clos en ce tombeau; "

an Italian version by a young Greek of Venice:

> " Piangete, O Veneri,
> Piangete, Amori,
> E voi piu teneri
> Leggiadir cori."

Of the little poem on Catullus' yacht, Sixte
Octavien had already published in 1579 a

collection of ten Latin parodies. Noël cites
thirteen others by German, French and Dutch
writers, making twenty-three in all, besides
various other French versions. Even more
popular proved the little ode urging Lesbia to
make hay while love's sun shines.[165] Noël
gives a list of thirty different French imitations in various meters. Some of them begin
thus:

(a) " Vivons pour nous aimer, ma charmante
            Lesbie,
        Pour enivrer nos cœurs du nectar des
            désirs; "

(b) " Aimons-nous, aimable Lesbie,
        Et laissons murmurer l'enviè; "

(c) " Vivons pour nous, O ma Lesbie;
        Cédons à nos tendres désirs; "

(d) " Aimons, Zélie,
        Durant les jours,
        Hélas! trop courts
        De notre vie; "

(e) " Vivons, O ma Julie!
        Jourons d'aimer toujours;
        Le printemps de la vie
        Est fait pour les amours;"

(f) " Cueillons les fleurs du printemps de la vie,
        Aimons, O ma Myrtis, vivons pour nous
            aimer."

The *epithalamia* (a favorite type with the
French and Italians) furnished inspiration to
many poets of each of those peoples, including
one by Buchanan for François and Mary
Stuart, one in Italian in which " Virginity "
addresses the bride, one by J. B. Rousseau,
another by de Barco, and still another by
Baour-Lormain. In Leonard's *Alexis* some of
the Catullian strophes in No. 61 are imitated.
Although few have had the courage to try
their hand on the *Attis*, there was a French
imitation with much variety of meter; and
an Italian named Pigna wrote a Latin poem
in Galliambics, on the metamorphosis of
Pitys into a pine tree. Among various French
epigrams, based on Catullus' assurance that
Lesbia loves him because she talks abusively
about him,[166] may be quoted that of Bernard:

" Glycère dit de moi *la rage* à tout moment.
    Je veux mourir, si Glycère ne m'aime!
    J'ignore la raison de ce caprice extreme:
    Mais je sais bien que j'eu parlé de même
    Et que je l'aime éperdument."

Another version, by Bussy de Rabutin, has
been translated into English by Theodore
Martin: [167]

" *Phillis pounds me with abuse,*
  Oh, her tongue's the very deuce!
  'Tis the way — quite new you'll own —
  Her regard and truth are shown.
  Yet what makes me think that she
  Is at heart in love with me,
  Is that with abuse I pound her,
  Yet adore her still, confound her! "

In addition to complete translations of his works, nearly one half of the poems in the Catullus collection have been, individually, translated, imitated, or parodied in French, some of them so often that the whole bulk of such literature is very considerable. The influence of these versions, complete and partial, upon the literature of a people possessed of the French ardent temperament is beyond our power to estimate; the spirit of Catullus permeates modern French and other modern literatures.

It is impossible here to carry the search throughout the wide reaches of all the European literatures. Moreover, as the distance from the original voice increases, the echoes often grow fainter. Although, as Pellissier says,[168] the " classic epoch " of French literature, for example, extends from the middle

of the sixteenth to the beginning of the nineteenth century, the critical spirit which began
to come in at the end of the sixteenth century
caused a decline in the eagerness with which
the *Pleiade* was followed, and, with the progress of scientific criticism, the attitude towards
the classics and their usefulness in shaping
the national literature of France shifted from
time to time. In Germany similar phases
succeeded each other. Goethe's interest in
Catullus, for example, may, perhaps, be di-
vined from one of his poems in the series
entitled, *Antiker Form sich nähernd,* in which
he incorporates the thought of the earlier
poet, as it had been expressed in the comparison between Lesbia and Quintia: [169]

"Was bedenklich Natur sonst unter Viele ver-
theilet,
    Gab sie mit reichlicher Hand Alles der Ein-
    zigen, ihr," etc.

" *All the divine perfections, which, whilere,*
    Nature in thrift doled out to many a fair,
She shower'd with liberal hand, thou peerless one,
    on thee;
And she that was so wondrously endowed,
    To whom a thousand noble knees were bow'd,
Gave all, love's perfect gift, her peerless self,
    to me." [170]

When in recent times Carducci voices his sensitive sympathy with the ancient poet's enthusiastic appreciation of the sensuous beauty of Sirmio and the Lago di Garda, we need no interpreter, to be sure, no industrious searcher for remote allusions or delicate parallels; and know that in the Italy of today the inspiration of Catullus is still effective upon poetic souls. Carducci loves his Catullus: [171]

" See *how green Sirmio laughs in the lake's lucid*
      waters,
  she the peninsula's flower! " [172]

  .   .   .   . [173]

" *here Valerius Catullus moored to the wet rocks,*
      of old,
  his frail pitched canoe,
  sat through the long days and watched in the
      waves, phosphorescent and tremulous,
  the eyes of his Lesbia;
  yea, and saw in those waves the changing moods
      of Lesbia,
  saw her perfidious smile,
  the while she beguiled with her charms, through
      darksome haunts of the town,[174]
  the princely nephews of Romulus.
  To *him from the humid depths sang forth the*
      nymph of the lake,
  ' *Come to us, Quintus Valerius!* ' "

But should one make a little *giro* through the
" harmonious numbers " of the French poets
of the nineteenth century, he would stop
occasionally, and, listening intently, wonder
just what the relation is of many a passage,
here and there, to a familiar Catullian thought
or beauty of expression. When Lamartine in
The Lake exclaims, — [175]

> " *Haste, then, to love! Seize happiness before*
> *The fleeting moments fly!*
> *Man has no haven here, and time no shore:*
> *Life flows, and we glide by!* "

it may be something more than merely the
Epicurean mood of Catullus [176] that the French
poet has caught. When Alfred de Musset, in
The Night in May, puts this question into the
mouth of the Muse:

> " *Say from what hand unnumbered lamps above*
> *Lighten by night and day in heavenly domes*
> *The holy oil of life and deathless love?* " [177]

perhaps Catullus' stars, looking down upon
the stolen sweets of human love,[178] were his
inspiration.

Was there a recollection of Catullus, meeting his Lesbia in transports of joy at the

home of his friend Allius,[179] flitting through the mind of Gautier when he penned this stanza? — [180]

> " Here is the bower that breathes the fragrance
>   Of clustering lilacs twined,
> Wherein, when weary of love's vagrance,
>   Together we reclined;
> Where, under coronals of flowers,
> We watched the flight of sultry hours."

Baudelaire perhaps was thinking of Catullus and of Lesbia's kisses [181] when he writes of

> " blue wastes of sky and desert sand
> That watch unmoved the sorrows of the world."

Theodore de Banville in *Medea* is only slightly varying the beautiful figure of Catullus in his first *epithalamium* [182], when he tells how

> " the wandering winds
>   .   .   .   .
> spread her tresses like a stream of light." [183]

It is the same desperate demand for love, though the loved one be untrustworthy, seen in Catullus, which Albert Glatigny utters, *In the Arbour:*

" Thine eyes are blue, but in the light thereof
    There seems a change, their look is dim and
      cold.
Yet, though thou liest, speak to me of love,
    My heart is sad and fain would be consoled."

Did Catulle Mendès have in mind the picture
of Cybele's lion at sunrise rounding up the
recreant Attis,[184] when in *The Curses of Hagar*
he describes the morning thus? —

" Then, in a sudden burst of wakening glory,
    Like a fierce lion from his lair outrun,
With golden mane ablaze and flanks all gory,
    On the red sky-line rose the splendid sun." [185]

Such hidden connections between the past and
the present are beautifully imaged in Gautier's poem on *Secret Affinities:* [186]

" Marble, and pearl, and rose, and dove,
    Decay and die. Time melts the stone,
The pearl dissolves, the flower of love
    Falls withered, and the bird is flown.

Their dust, through changes manifold
    Dispersed, earth's deep alembic brings
To enrich the universal mould
    Whence Nature shapes all beauteous things.

By *transmutation slow and strange,*
  In divers forms they recompose;
White marbles into white limbs change,
  On rosy lips reblooms the rose.

Once more the dove with amorous coo
  The fresh young heart of love beguiles,
And pearls in clustered teeth renew
  Their whiteness wreathed in radiant smiles.
        .   .   .   .
Thou before whom I thrill and glow!
  What wave, what shrine, what dome, what
    bower,
Knew us, in ages long ago,
  As pearl or marble, dove or flower? "

So, also, in the mysterious connection between
Catullus and us of today we can see the ever-
recurring miracle of a revival of an ancient
appreciation of life and a re-incarnation of
the passionate intensity, sensuousness and
genuineness of Catullus in the poetic expression of later days. At times the noble heritage of classic thought, form and spirit is un-
consciously applied by the touch of genius to
an unpolished gem of the human imagination,
transmuting it into a new jewel of wondrous
beauty.

VI. CATULLUS IN ENGLAND

FROM John Gower's day to our own, English literature has drawn copiously, either directly or indirectly, on classical themes and models. The scholarship of the great English schools and universities, which has colored the whole fabric of English thought, has been prevailingly and preëminently classical. Of the important gifts which Catullus in particular has bestowed on our English-speaking civilization we can trace abundant proofs. Many translations, exerting an incalculable influence, have admirably put his beauty before the English people. English scholarship through the person of Robinson Ellis is responsible for the outstanding edition of our poet, while many other English scholars have made valuable contributions to our knowledge and appreciation of his work and its significance to us. Imitations, parodies, and passages suggested by Catullus abound in the English poetry of the last half millennium. Men prominent in church and state, as well as in the world of letters, have gladly acknowledged their delight in the tenderness, fervor and beauty of the Roman lyrist of long ago.

It is a well-known fact that Lord Macaulay, that brilliant master of English style, was in the habit of reading and re-reading his ancient classics. In his copy of Catullus was written: "Finished Catullus August 3d, 1835. An admirable poet. No Latin writer is so Greek. The simplicity, the pathos, the perfect grace, which I find in the great Athenian models are all in Catullus, and in him alone of the Romans." [187] Macaulay's biographer refers to the fact that all his "thoughts were often for weeks together more in Latium and Attica than in Middlesex," and to his enthusiastic and sympathetic appreciation of the classics, telling how he "cried over Homer with emotion, and over Aristophanes with laughter, and could not read the *De Corona* even for the twentieth time without striking his clenched fist at least once a minute on the arm of his easy chair." Towards the close of his life, after many readings of the poet, he writes thus: [188] "I have pretty near learned all that I like best in Catullus. He grows on me with intimacy. One thing he has — I do not know whether it belongs to him or to something in myself — but there are chords of my mind which he touches as nobody else does. The first lines of *Miser Catulle;* [189] the lines to Cornificius, written evidently from a sick-bed; [190] and part of the poem beginning *Si qua recordanti,*[191] affect me more than I can explain. They always move me to tears." And, speaking of Martial, he adds, " Sometimes he runs Catullus himself hard," showing that he did not fail to read and value the epigrammatic part of the Catullus collection. Mr. Gladstone used to beguile his weariness, in the midst of cares of state, by making translations of Catullus, as well as of other Latin poets, — for example, of Catullus' fifty-first *carmen,* the opening stanza of which he renders as follows:

> " H*im rival to the Gods I place,*
> H*im loftier yet, if loftier be,*
> W*ho, Lesbia, sits before thy face,*
> W*ho listens and who looks on thee.*"

Tennyson's visit to Sirmio was like a pilgrimage to a real shrine of poetry; for, as Mr. Slater remarks, he went " to the cenotaph of

Catullus as Catullus had come to the grave of his brother." That among the recreations of such a "country clergyman" as Thomas Twining,[192] in the eighteenth century, was that of parodying Catullus is seen from his clever verses about his boat on the parsonage pond:[193]

> "*The boat which here you see, my friends,*
> *Sharp as a needle at both ends,*
> *A bean-shell for my wife and me,*
> *Deep-loaded when it carries three;*
>
> . . . .
>
> *Protests and vows, and, if you'll have it,*
> *Is ready to make affidavit,*
> *That she's the fleetest little thing*
> *That ever flew on wooden wing.*"

So to people of different ranks, occupations, and tasks there has seemed to come a universal appeal in the poetry of Catullus.

Yet it is clear that Catullus was not one of the first Latin poets to become popular in England. This is doubtless due in some degree to the partial eclipse which he suffered on the continent during the Middle Ages. Virgil, Horace and Ovid were widely known in Europe when Catullus was in obscurity, and they became popular in England before he was generally known to the English public. It is significant that in Miss Palmer's official list of *English Editions and Translations of Greek and Latin Classics Printed before 1641* [194] appears but a single entry under "Catullus," — "an edition of the *Phasellus ille* poem with such parodies on it as were then extant, edited, with the annotations of eminent scholars, and the addition of certain other poems of similar nature, by Sixtus Octavianus, and printed at York in the year 1579." But the same list contains the titles of thirty-five editions or translations of the whole or part of the works of Horace! Another reason for this discrepancy between the popularity of Horace and that of Catullus in the early period is emphasized by Mr. Berdan in his book on *Early Tudor Poetry*,[195] namely a "line of cleavage between the types of humanism developed south and north of the Alps," — Catullus being the favorite type in Italy, Horace in the northern countries. Though this is partly due, perhaps, to the belated re-discovery of Catullus in the four-teenth century in Italy, the more important reason lies, probably, as found by Mr. Berdan, in the different temper of the peoples. " The fire and passion of Catullus found a congenial soil in Italy." " The cold, restrained, northern nature felt more at ease with the philosophy of Horace." " In Tudor England, humanism was a serious, moral, reflective force."

In spite of such influences, Catullus began to make himself felt even in very early English literature. Often the transmission of thought was indirect, even through several media. Chaucer may have known Petrarch himself, when in Italy; and it is conceivable that he had made a direct acquaintance with the poetry of Catullus. But it is altogether probable that all he knew about the Ariadne episode in the *Peleus and Thetis* came through the better known Ovid rather than through Catullus himself. The story is told in the *Legende of Goode Women* as it occurs in the *Heroides*,[196] and to that version the poet directly refers:

" I*n hys Epistil Naso telleth alle.*"

But this, as we have already seen, is one of four places where Ovid directly borrowed the story and many of its special features from the *Peleus and Thetis* of Catullus; and it is easy to see there [197] the picture which Chaucer thus reflects: [198]

> " And *to the stronde barefote she wente,*
>   *And cryede, ' Theseus! myn herte swete!*
>   *Where be ye, that I may not wyth you mete?*
>   *And myghte thus with bestes ben yslayne.'*
>   *The holowe roches answerde hir agayne.*
>   *No man she sawe, and yet shone the mone,*
>   *And hye upon a rokke she wente sone,*
>   *And saw hys barge saylynge in the sea."*

It is also interesting to notice that in *The Parlement of Fowles,* among the many terse characterizations of birds, Chaucer speaks of

> " The *sparwe, Venus sone*," [199]

an idea that may have come to him from the *Sparrow* song of Catullus. Even before this, in the *Harleian* lyrics, we may read:

> " I *would I were a thrustle cock,*
>   A *bountyng or a laverok,*
>   *Sweet bride.*
>   *Between her kirtle and her smock*
>   I *would me hide;"* —

lines which, remarks Mr. Waller, in *The Cambridge History of English Literature,*[200]

[142]

"form a link in the long chain that binds Catullus to the Elizabethan and Jacobean lyrists." It may be added, as a matter of significance, that in the French *Romance of the Rose,* on which Chaucer's poem was based, Tibullus, Catullus, Ovid and Gallus are mentioned as inspiring poets in love themes.

But if these early Catullian reminiscences in English literature are of relatively trifling importance, — with the coming of the classical Renaissance from the continent, before the end of the fifteenth century, a full knowledge of Catullus appears. Linacre, Colet, Latimer, Erasmus, Grocyn, and their contemporaries, fresh from France and Italy and direct contact with the new humanism, inspired a general desire to know classical literature more thoroughly; and the result was great and profound upon the literature and thought of England. John Skelton, poet laureate in the first years of the new sixteenth century, who called himself the British Catullus in the couplet, —

"Ite, Britannorum lux O radiosa, Britannum
  Carmina nostra pium vestrum celebrate Catullum!"

uses the two poems on Lesbia's sparrow as a
peg upon which to hang a curious mélange of
poetry and satire in his *Philip Sparrow*. How
well he knew the originals is palpable from
such verses as these:

> " Alas! my heart it slayeth,
> My Philip's doleful death!
> When I remember it,
> How prettily it would sit,
> Many times and oft,
> Upon my finger aloft.
> I played with him Tittle-tattle
> And fed him with my spattle,
> With his bill between my lips.
>
> .   .   .
>
> And, many times and oft
> Between my breasts soft
> It would lie and rest,
> It was proper and prest."

With this one need compare, for example, but
a stanza or two of Cranstoun's versions of the
originals:

> " Sparrow! my darling's joy!
> With whom she's wont to toy,
> With whom some warm breast-nestling nook to fill;
> And, to frolic combat firing

Thee her finger-tip desiring,
To provoke the pricking peckings of thy bill.
. . . .
For 'twas a honey'd pet,
And knew her well as yet
A mother by her daughter e'er was known:
Never from her bosom stray'd he,
Hopping hither, thither play'd he,
Ever piped and chirped his song to her alone."

This enthusiasm over classical literature moved on apace through the sixteenth century, and we must reckon both with the direct study and imitation of Greek and Latin models and with the even greater indirect influence from the Italian, and the French, Renaissance, with Petrarch, Ariosto, Marot, Ronsard, and the rest of the *Pleiade*, and with the throng of students and scholars who were passing back and forth between London and Rome and Paris. The serious writers of this period repeatedly mention Catullus as a leading Roman poet, worthy of imitation. Roger Ascham in the *Scholemaster* groups " Lucretius, Catullus, Virgil, and Horace " as " most excellent Poetes, deserving well of the Latin tong; " and elsewhere in the same work he recognizes " how Virgil himself in the story

[145]

of Dido doth wholly imitate Catullus in the
like matter of Ariadna." William Webbe in
his *Discourse of English Poetrie* names as
" rare and excellent Poets " who wrote of
lighter subjects, " Propertius, Tibullus, Catullus, and divers whom Ovid speaketh of in
divers places of his works." Webbe defends
Catullus against adverse criticism in two
other passages in this critical work. Sir
Thomas Elyot did the same in *The Gouver-
nour*. Sir George Puttenham in his treatise *Of
Poets and Poesy* names Catullus three times,
and in the chapter on " The Manner of Re-
joysings at Marriages and Weddings " bases
his description indubitably upon the 61st and
62d poems of Catullus. Richard Carew on
The Excellency of the English Tongue compares Catullus to Shakespeare (presumably
with the *Sonnets* in mind). Francis Meres in
A Comparison of English Poets speaks of the
eminence of Catullus in both lyric and epigrammatic poetry, and refers to Virgil's
imitation of his Ariadne story. Thomas
Campion in his *Observations in the Art of
English Poesie* talks of the " Hendicasillables "
of Catullus. Samuel Daniel in *A Defense of
Ryme* quotes the 22d of Catullus in con-

firmation of the thought that we are poor critics of our own work.

Meanwhile English lyric poets and poetry were multiplying, and showed, throughout, the classical influence. The sonnets, songs and eclogues of Wyatt, Surrey, Googe and Sidney are crowded with classical names, themes and conceits; yet often their Petrarchian form partially conceals the real original. The lyrics of Wyatt, for instance, are full of more or less disguised re-creations of the pictures or the emotions of Catullus, though Wyatt may not have always himself recognized their source. Here is the Catullian comparison of love to a mountain stream: [201]

> " *From these hie hills as when a spring doth fall,*
> *It trilleth downe with still and suttle course,*
> *Of this and that it gathers ay and shall*
> *Till it have just down-flowed to streame and force:*
> *Then at the fote it rageth over all.*
> *So fareth love, when it hath tane a source.*"

Whether it is the lover, disillusioned with regard to his lady's constancy,[202] or the mood of Catullus trying to harden his heart in order to break away from Lesbia, but secretly hop-

ing he will fail,[203] or the thought of the unap-
preciated kiss,[204] Catullus seems to live again
in the lyrics of Wyatt. And here is reënacted
the old inconsistent heart struggle of the Roman lover: [205]

" I *wish to perysh, yet I ask for helth,*
  I *love another, and thus I hate my selfe.*"

Sir Philip Sidney's method of expressing
the same thought in *Astrophel and Stella* is
more highly figurative:

" *On Cupid's bow how are my heart-strings bent!*
That see my wrack, and yet embrace the same.
When most I glory, then I feel most shame.
I willing run, yet while I run, repent."

When, however, Sidney wished to emphasize
the fickleness of woman, he frankly translated Catullus, No. 70:

" ' *Unto nobody,*' *my woman saith,* ' *she had*
    rather a wife be
Than to myself; not though Jove grew a suitor
    of hers.'
These be her words, but a woman's words to a
    love that is eager,
In wind or water's streame do require to be writ."

[148]

More than one whole type of English poetry can be traced directly back to Catullus. This is true of the madrigal. For what is commonly regarded as the first English madrigal, *La Verginella*, by William Byrd,[206] which appeared in *Musica Transalpina* in 1588, is a mere translation from the second *epithalamium* of Catullus,[207] through the medium of Ariosto, whose debt we have already noted:

I

" The fair young virgin is like the rose untainted
  In garden fair, while tender stalk doth bear it,
  Sole, and untoucht, with no resort acquainted;
  No shepherd nor his flock doth once come near it:
  Th' air, full of sweetness, the morning fresh
        depainted;
  The earth, the water, with all their favours
        cheer it;
  Dainty young gallants, and ladies most desired,
  Delight to have therewith their heads and breasts
        attired.

II

But not so soon, from green stock where it
        growed,
  The same is pluckt, and from the branch removed;
  As lost is all from heaven and earth that flowed;
  Both favour, grace and beauty best beloved.

[149]

The virgin fair, that hath the flower bestowed
(Which more than life to guard, it her behoved)
Loseth her praise, and is no more desired
Of those, that late unto her love aspired."

In passing it may be remarked that a study
of old English songs would probably yield
various curious reminiscences of our poet. So,
for example, the third stanza of the song,
Come Ye Young Men, in Chappell's *Popular
Music of the Olden Time,* begins with a
Catullian theme.[208]

The *Epithalamium* also, in its literary history, as we trace it from Catullus down through
Seneca's *Medea,* the *Stella and Violentilla* of
Statius, Claudian, Apollinaris Sidonius, George
Buchanan, J. B. Rousseau, Spenser, Ben Jonson, Donne, Herrick, and even the end of
Tennyson's *In Memoriam,* derives its inspiration and much of its form from the examples
of this type in the old Latin poet. So far as
Spenser is concerned, his *Epithalamium*
glitters with jewels gathered from Catullus.

" *Now is my love all ready forth to come*
Let all the virgins therefore well awayt;
And ye fresh boyes, that tend upon her groome,
Prepare yourselves; for he is coming strayt.

. . . .

The whyles the boyes run up and downe the
    street,
Crying aloud with strong confused noyce,
As if it were one voyce.
Hymen, io Hymen, Hymen, they do shout;

.   .   .   .

Loe! where she comes along with portly pace,
Lyke Phoebe, from her chamber of the East,

.   .   .   .

Her long loose yellow locks like golden wyre.

.   .   .   .

Hast thee, O fayrest planet, to thy home,
Within the Westerne fome:
The tyred steedes long since have need of rest.
Long though it be, at last I see it gloome,
And the bright evening-star with golden creast,
Appeare out of the East.

.   .   .   .

Now cease, ye damsels, your delights forepast;
Enough it is that all the day was youres:
Now day is doen, and night is nighing fast,
Now bring the bryde into the brydall boures."

The *Faerie Queene* of Spenser was of course
built largely on the *Orlando Furioso* of
Ariosto. We have already seen something of
the debt of Ariosto to Catullus. It is through
Ariosto and Tasso that the Catullian simile of

the maiden and the rose is transformed into this beautiful song: [209]

" Ah! see, who so fayre thing doest faine to see,
In springing flowre the image of thy day!
Ah! see the virgin rose, how sweetly shee
Doth first peepe foorth with bashful modestee,
That fairer seemes the lesse ye see her may!
Lo! see soone after, how more bold and free
Her bared bosome she doth broad display;
Lo! see soone after, how she fades and falles
    away!

. . . .

So passeth, in the passing of a day,
Of mortall life the leafe, the bud, the flowre;
Ne more doth florish after first decay,
That earst was sought to deck both bed and
    bowre
Of many a ladie and many a paramowre!
Gather therefore the rose whilest yet is prime,
For soone comes age that will her pride deflowre."

Other Spenserian figures, run in the Catullian mold, might be mentioned, — for example:

" The charming smiles, that rob sence from the
    hart," [210]

and the familiar reckoning of Lesbia's kisses: [211]

"*More loth to number with how many eyes
High heaven beholds sad lovers' nightly thiev-
eries.*"

When Spenser pictures the Graces, who

"*seemed all to sing,
Hymen Iö Hymen! dauncing all around,*" [212]

or how Peleus

"*was with Thetis love assaid,
Great Nereus his daughter and his joy,*" [213]

we need not speculate long as to the origin of his inspiration about these mythological personages.

It is hardly worth while to tarry over such trifles as Gascoigne's *The Praise of Philip Sparrow,* in which that now familiar birdling's virtues are elaborated, or Turberville's complaint of *The Pine to the Mariner,* where we are reminded of the source, namely, Catullus' *Yacht* and its subsequent adventures. For with the ripening of the Elizabethan age more significant phenomena demand our attention. The idea that Shakespeare was not well educated is no longer tenable.[214] Though no such connoisseur of the classics as Ben Jonson, it is clear that he had a direct or indirect acquaintance with a considerable number of Latin, French and Italian authors, to say nothing of Plutarch. The fact that in his day there were not as yet available any English translations of Catullus is important. Yet, despite his perfectly natural devotion to the story-telling Ovid and Livy, notable reminiscences of Catullus, also, can be discovered in Shakespeare. The expression of Catullus, 'what a woman says to her eager lover deserves to be written on the wind and on the rushing water,' had undoubtedly passed through many hands before it reached the great English dramatist. Philip Sidney had rendered it:

" but a woman's words to a love that is eager,
In wind or water's streame do require to be writ."

Beaumont and Fletcher, his contemporaries, in *Philaster,* wrote:

" All your better deeds
Shall be in water writ, but this in marble."

Perhaps the phrase came to Shakespeare through Sidney; at any rate, in *Henry VIII,*[215] we read:

" *Men's evil manners live in brass; their virtues*
  We write in water."

Again, the figure of matrimony typified by a
pliant vine entwining an elm, which Catullus
gave to posterity in each of his famous
epithalamia,[216] popularized through Ovid and
other Roman writers, and their medieval imitators, is frequently met in the Elizabethan
period. Sidney in his *Arcadia* speaks of

" *The honest bridegroome and the bashfull Bride,*
  Whose loves may ever bide
  Like to the elme and vine
  With mutuall embracements them to twyne."

Thomas Kyd in *The Spanish Tragedy* says:

" *Nay then my arms are large and strong withal:*
  Thus elms by vines are compass'd till they fall."

Daniel in *The Complaint of Rosamund* writes:

" *And as the vine married unto the Elme*
  With strict embraces, so doth he infold it."

Shakespeare employs the figure twice, — quite
simply in the *Comedy of Errors:*[217]

" *Thou art an elm, my husband, I a vine,*"

[155]

and more elaborately in *A Midsummer Night's Dream*, when Titania says fondly to Bottom: [218]

" *Sleep thou, and I will wind thee in my arms:*
 So doth the woodbine the sweet honeysuckle
 Gently entwist; the female ivy so
 Enrings the barky fingers of the elm."

Love's Labour Lost [219] and even Hamlet's [220] —

" *The undiscover'd country, from whose bourne*
 No traveler returns,"

may be under debt to Catullus.

Mr. Macnaghten has compared the course of Shakespeare's love for " the dark lady of the sonnets," who, he has no doubt, was Mary Fitton, with that of Catullus for Lesbia, and sees a remarkable parallel between the two experiences, — the beauty and aristocracy of the lady, her unfaithfulness to both husband and lover, and the devotion of the lovers, even to the point of condoning the gravest of faults. Certainly many of the *Sonnets* of Shakespeare sound like variations on the theme of the bitter-sweet of love as Catullus learned it from his Lesbia.

In spite of the strong classical element in

the English poetry of the sixteenth century, the influence of Petrarch, Ronsard, and the *Pleiade* was dominant, especially in the lyric. But with the dawn of the seventeenth century, there is, as Mr. Moorman has expressed it,[221] " a return to the greater directness and less etherial temper of the classical lyric of Anacreon, Catullus and Horace. In the drama ' the classical lyric,' as attuned by Ben Jonson, becomes supreme. . . . And when we turn from the lyrics in the dramas to those which were sung in the banqueting chamber at Whitehall, the influence of Jonson is again felt; . . . it is everywhere felt in the lyrics of Herrick and Carew, and its presence is likewise felt in those of Cartwright, Randolph and Waller." An important element in this new and strong classical influence is that of Catullus. It is seen constantly in the leading poets of the period. Although the first notable representative of the new movement was perhaps John Donne, yet signs of it appeared in his earlier contemporary dramatists and lyrists. When George Chapman, the translator of Homer, completed the likewise classically-inclined Christopher Marlowe's *Hero and Leander* at the end of the sixteenth century, he incorporated in it a striking imitation of parts of the second *epithalamium* of Catullus: [222]

> " Rise, youths! Love's rite claims more than
>   banquets; rise!
>
> .   .   .   .   .   .
>
> Rise, virgins! let fair nuptial love enfold
> Your fruitless breasts: the maidenheads ye hold
> Are not your own, but parted are;
> Part in disposing them your parents share,
> And that a third part is: so must ye save
> Your loves a third, and you your thirds must
>   have."

Marlowe himself, in *The Passionate Shepherd to his Love*, sang:

> " Come live with me and be my love,
>   And we will all the pleasures prove
>   That hills and vallies, dales and fields,
>   Woods or steepy mountain yields.
>
> .   .   .   .   .   .
>
> And I will make thee beds of roses
>   And a thousand fragrant posies,
>   A cup of flowers and a kirtle
>   Embroidered all with leaves of myrtle."

which is very much in the spirit of Catullus.

Sir John Davies did not hesitate to go the limit in imitating the scurrilous attacks of the worst Catullian epigrams, and the odious personal characteristics of the notorious Ameana, Rufus, Gellius, and Aemilius are predicated of later objects of poetic spleen, now dubbed " Gella," " Septimius," or " Silla." Thomas Campion, who added further charm to his lyrics by setting them to original music in many cases, first published, after spending several years at Cambridge, a book of Latin poems including many epigrams addressed to such familiar names as Acme, Calvus and Cinna, which must have drawn much inspiration from Catullus. The first song in his *Book of Airs* is a famous paraphrase of Catullus' fifth lyric:

" *My sweetest Lesbia, let us live and love;*
 And though the sager sort our deeds reprove,
 Let us not weigh them: heaven's great lamps
    do dive
 Into their west, and straight again revive:
 But when as once set is our little light
 Then must we sleep one ever-during night."

Here he leaves the original, but recurs to it in one of the *Light Conceits of Lovers:*[223]

> " *Sooner may you count the stars,*
> *And number hail down pouring,*
> *Tell the osiers of the Thames,*
> *Or Goodwin Sands devouring,*
> *Than the thick-showered kisses here*
> *Which now thy tired lips must bear.*"

Campion elaborates upon Catullus' futile attempt at renunciation: [224]

> " *Harden now thy tired heart, with more than*
> *flinty rage!*
> *Ne'er let her false tears henceforth thy constant*
> *grief assuage!* " etc.

In the *Second Book of Airs* the couplet,

> " *My object now must be the air,*
> *To write in water words of fire,*"

reminds us of Catullus, No. 70; and in the *Third Book of Airs*, No. 17 recalls Catullus, No. 32; and Campion's No. 29 his No. 76. The *Masque at the Marriage of the Lord Hayes* is full of reminiscences of the Catullian *epithalamia*. The version of *Vivamus, mea Lesbia*, in Corkine's *Second Book of Lyricks*, beginning,

> " *My dearest mistrisse, let us live and love,*
> *And care not what old doting fools reprove,*"

is believed by Vivian to be really Campion's
work.

John Donne's passionate intensity and
genuineness impressed his contemporaries as
well as his successors as being in the manner of
the impetuous Catullus. In *Lovers' Infinite-
ness,* he protests:

" If *yet I have not all thy love,*
  Dear, I shall never have it all,
  I cannot breathe one other sigh, to move,
  Nor can intreat one other tear to fall,
  And all my treasure, which should purchase thee,
  Sighs, tears, and oaths, and letters I have spent."

Daniel's variation on the love theme is as
follows:

" *Let's love, the sun doth set and rise again*
  But when as our short light
Comes once to set, it makes eternal night,"

Michael Drayton writes thus:

  " *One kiss in two let's breathe!*
    Confounded with the touch,
  But half words let us speak!
    Our lips employed so much,
  Until we both grow weak:

[161]

> *With sweetness of thy breath,*
> *O smother me to death!*
> *Long let our joys be such!"*

But the most eminent classicist in English letters in those times was Ben Jonson. A sound classical scholar, a careful translator, well read in both Greek and Latin literature, he was so well recognized by his fellows as the champion of classical learning that the memorial verses known as *Jonsonus Virbius* speak of his lyrics as

> *"Tuned to the highest key of ancient Rome,*
> *Returning all her music with his own."*

His eminence has been described thus: " Jonson in his day stood alone in his championship and first in his conscious theory of art based upon scholarship." It was to Anacreon, Catullus and Horace that Jonson was most indebted for subject and form in his lyrics.[225] The first proof of his intimacy with Catullus that would come to the mind of every one of his disciples is, of course, the song from *Volpone,* based on Catullus' fifth ode:

> *" Come, my Celia, let us prove*
> *While we can the sports of love;*

Time will not be ours forever,
He at length our good will sever;
Spend not thou his gifts in vain.
Suns that set may rise again;
But if once we lose this light,
'Tis with us perpetual night.
Why should we defer our joys?
Fame and rumor are but toys."

And in another song, *The Forest*, we are again reminded of Catullus:

" *Kiss, and score up wealthy sums*
On my lips, thus hardly sundred,
While you breathe. First give a hundred,
Then a thousand, then another
Hundred, then unto the tother
Add a thousand, and so more:
Till you equal with the store,
All the grass that Rumney yields,
Or the sands in Chelsea fields,
Or the drops in silver Thames,
Or the stars that gild his streams,
In the silent summer-nights,
When youths ply their stoln delights.
That the curious may not know
How to tell them as they flow,
And the envious, when they find
What this number is, be pin'd."

In an ode justifying his praise of Celia, recalling the galaxy of fair classical ladies, after
mention of Helen and Homer, Sappho and
Phaon, he comes at length to ask:

> " Was *Lesbia sung by learn'd Catullus?*
> *Or Delia's graces by Tibullus?* "

and, after mentioning Petrarch, Ronsard, Sidney and Constable, he concludes:

> " And *shall not* I *my Celia bring*
> W*here men may see whom* I *do sing?* "

Chance reminiscences of Catullus occur every
now and then in Jonson's dramas. In *Cynthia's Revels* [226] the Perfumer advises Amor-
phus: " Taste, smell; I assure you, sir, pure
benjamin, the only spirited scent that ever
awaked a Neapolitan nostril. You would wish
yourself all nose for the love on't." In *The
Underwoods* [227] he recurs to the Catullian
figure for female inconstancy:

> " Are *vows so cheap with women? or the matter*
> W*hereof they are made, that they are writ in*
> *water,*
> A*nd blown away with wind?* "

Even in the most familiar gem that Jonson
ever polished, his

" Drink to me only with thine eyes,"

we catch, perhaps, a reflection of Catullus,
as he sings:

> *" But might I of Jove's nectar sip,*
> *I would not change for thine."* [228]

Jonson's various *epithalamia* are deeply indebted to Catullus not merely for their general
ideas and progress of thought, but also con-
tinually for the exact expression of it. In
the dialogue of *The Masque of Hymen*,
Reason exclaims:

> *" Up, youths! hold up your lights in air,*
> *And shake abroad their flaming hair."* [229]

Indeed, the very plan of having a dialogue
between Hymen and Reason corresponds to
the arguments for and against wedlock, in
Catullus. The *epithalamium* in this masque,
of which only the first stanza, we are informed,
was actually recited on the occasion of its
presentation, is a clever paraphrase of Catullus' first poem of this type, and is well adapted
in its short lines and its stanza arrangement
to represent the original. A stanza may be
quoted:

" Help, youths and virgins, help to sing
  The Prize which Hymen here doth bring,
  And did so lately rap
  From forth the mother's lap,
  To place her by that side
  Where she must long abide.
  On Hymen, Hymen call,
  This night is Hymen's all."

To quote one more example, — in *The Barriers* the debate is carried on by Truth and Opinion, who introduce two of the famous similes from Catullus' second *epithalamium*, as follows: [230]

OPINION,

" Look how a flower that close in closes grows,
  Hid from rude cattle, bruisèd with no plows,
  Which the air doth stroke, sun strengthen,
      showers shoot higher,
  It many youths, and many maids desire;
  The same, when cropt by cruel hand 'tis wither'd,
  No youths at all, no maidens have desired.

. . . . . .

TRUTH,

  Virgins, O virgins, to sweet Hymen yield,
  For as a lone vine, in a naked field,
  Never extols her branches, never bears
  Ripe grapes, but with a headlong heaviness wears

> *Her tender body, and her highest sprout*
> *Is quickly levell'd with her fading root;*
> *By whom no husbandman, no youths will dwell;*
> *But if by fortune, she be married well*
> *To the elm her husband, many husbandmen*
> *And many youths inhabit by her then."*

Though there may not be conscious imitation of Catullus in the verses of Thomas Carew, yet he was as ardent a lover. In the spirit of Catullus,[231] he urged prompt enjoyment of life's fleeting pleasures:

> "*Oh then be wise, and whilst your season*
> *Affords you days for sport, do reason:*
> *Spend not in vain your life's short hour,*
> *But crop in time your beauty's flow'r:*
> *Which will away, and doth together*
> *Both bud and fade, both blow and wither;"*

and after bitter troubles, like Catullus,[232] he prayed for relief:

> "*Then, for pity, either stir*
> *Up the fire of love in her,*
> *That alike both flames may shine,*
> *Or else quite extinguish mine."*

But the Wind which he addressed did not hear his petition, and ultimately, like his original, he cast off the heartless one:

> "No tears, Celia, now shall win
>   My resolv'd heart to return." [233]

William Drummond begs for a single kiss, with the plea that he will, though equally ardent, not be so greedy as Catullus:

> "Though I with strange desire
>   To kiss those rosy lips am set on fire,
>   Yet will I cease to crave
>   Sweet kisses in such store,
>   As he who long before
>   In thousands them from Lesbia did receive.
>   Sweetheart, but one more kiss,
>   And I by that sweet bliss
>   Even swear to cease to importune you more."

Drummond has two poems inspired by the wail of Catullus for Lesbia's sparrow. The shorter one, *On the Death of a Linnet*, dwells upon the inexorability of the grim Reaper:

> "If cruel death had ears,
>   Or could be pleas'd by songs,
>   This wing'd musician had liv'd many years,
>   And Nisa mine had never wept these wrongs:
>
>   .   .   .   .
>
>   But Death, who nothing spares, and nothing
>   hears,
>   As he doth kings, kill'd it, O grief! O tears!"

The other, *Phillis, On the Death of the Sparrow,* approaches nearer to Catullus; as for example:

" No *more with trembling limbs shall he attend*
His *watchful mistress. Would my life could end!*
No *more shall I hear him chirp pretty lays;*

    .   .   .   .

To *touch or wrong his tail if any dar'd,*
He *pinch'd their fingers, and against them warr'd:*
Then *might that crest be seen shake up and down,*
Which *fixed was unto his little crown."*

References to the *Sparrow* song are frequent. Matthew Prior refers to it in his *Turtle and Sparrow,* in which a parallel thought is spun out with much prolixity, and the source of his inspiration is finally revealed:

" As *sure as Lesbia's Sparrow I,*
    Thou, *sure as Prior's Dove, must die."*

The Priorian echo of the Catullian *Vivamus, mea Lesbia,* appears in *An Ode to Celia:*

" Haste, *Celia, haste, while youth invites,*
    Obey *kind Cupid's present voice;*
Fill *every sense with soft delights,*
    And *give thy soul a loose to joys:*
Let *millions of repeated blisses prove*
That *thou all kindness art, and I all love."*

[169]

William Cartwright, too, has a version of the *Sparrow* song, in which he dwells on the bird's pretty ways. A few verses will give an idea of the style:

> " He *from my lip*
> W*ould moisture sip,*
> He *would from my trencher feed,*
> T*hen would hop, and then would run,*
> And *cry Philip when he had done;*
> O *whose heart can choose but bleed?*
> O *how eager would he fight!*
> And *ne'er hurt, though he did bite.*"

Cartwright also utters in lyric style in six irregular stanzas the complaint of Ariadne, " as she sits on a rock in the island of Naxos," beginning:

> " T*heseus! O Theseus hark! but yet in vain,*
> Alas *deserted I complain.*"

It continued to be popular with these poets to try their hand on Catullus' *Vivamus, mea Lesbia.* Richard Crashaw's version runs thus:

> " Come, *and let us live my dear,*
> Let *us love, and never fear*
> W*hat the sourest fathers say:*
>
> .   .   .   .   .   .
>
> Brightest *Sol, that dies today,*

Lives again as blithe tomorrow;
But if we, dark sons of sorrow,
Set, O! then how long a night
Shuts the eyes of our short light!
Then let amorous kisses dwell
On our lips, begin and tell
A thousand and a hundred score,
An hundred and a thousand more,

. . . . . .

Till another thousand smother
That, and that wipe off another.
Thus at last, when we have numb'red
Many a thousand, many a hundred;
We'll confound the reckoning quite,
And lose ourselves in wild delight:
While our joys so multiply
As shall mock the envious eye."

Alexander Brome's version begins as follows:

" My Lesbia, let us live and love,
    Let crabbed age talk what it will;
The sun, though down, returns above,
    But we, once dead, must be so still.
Kiss me a thousand times, and then
    Give me a hundred kisses more:
Now kiss a thousand times again,
    Then t'other hundred as before.
Come, a third thousand, and to those
    Another hundred kisses fix;

[171]

That done, to make the sweeter close,
  We'll millions of kisses mix,
And huddle them together so,
  That we ourselves shan't know how many;
And others can't their number know,
  If we should envied be by any." etc.

In the vivid imagination of Crashaw, a tear from the eye of his sweet Mary is to be exalted, even as was the lock cut from Berenice's hair; this is surely a classic conceit:

" *O 'tis not a tear,*
  'Tis a star about to drop
From thine eye its sphere;
  The sun will stoop and take it up.

  .   .   .   .   .   .

  Thus carried up on high,
  (For to Heaven thou must go)
  Sweetly shalt thou lie,
  And in soft slumbers bathe thy woe;
  Till the singing orbs awake thee,
  And one of their bright chorus make thee."

The favorite figure for fickleness [234] appears again, mayhap in disguise, in Sherburne's little poem, *The Broken Faith:*

"Lately by clear Thames's side,
Fair Lycoris I espied
With the pen of her white hand
These words printing on the sand:
'None Lycoris doth approve
But Mirtillo for her love.'
Ah false nymph! those words were fit
In sand only to be writ:
For the quickly rising streams
Of oblivion, and the Thames,
In a little moment's stay
From the shore washed clean away
What thy hand had there impressed,
And Mirtillo from thy breast."

Evidently he knew other Catullian conceits.
For example, in *Love's Arithmetic* we meet
the familiar reckoning:

"Equal to these sandy grains
Is the number of my pains:

.   .   .   .

Many as the earth hath leaves,
Are the griefs my heart receives;
And the stars which heaven inspires
Reckon my consuming fires.

.   .   .   .

We will count our griefs and blisses,
Thousand torments, thousand kisses."

Thomas Randolph, in what his editor, Hazlitt, calls a "somewhat warm production," *A Pastoral Courtship*, after a good deal of persuasive wooing, reaches at length the limits of Catullus' rapture:

> "*Now let us kiss. Would you be gone?*
> *Manners at least allows me one.*
> *Blush you at this? pretty one, stay,*
> *And I will take that kiss away.*
> *Thus with a second, and that too*
> *A third wipes off; so will we go*
> *To numbers that the stars outrun,*
> *And all the atoms in the sun.*"

Edmund Waller sounds the old note of fleeting joys, as he sings *To Phyllis*. This may be as old as Anacreon, it may be Epicurean, but Catullus had given it immortal literary expression. When he turns to Virgil, he chooses to translate the complaint of Dido, which, as we have seen, goes back to the Ariadne episode of Catullus.

The note of disappointment is often heard in the poetry of Abraham Cowley. Under such titles as *Inconstancy, The Vain Love, The Despair, All-Over Love, The Heart Fled Again, Coldness, Love's Ingratitude, The Dis-*

sembler, The Separation, his verses betray many of the Catullian moods. At last, in *Love Given Over,* he announces his purpose of renunciation, in essentially the words of Catullus: [235]

> " *Leave, wretched Cowley! leave*
> *Thyself with shadows to deceive;*
> *Think that already lost which thou must never*
> *gain.*"

In his essay, *Of Solitude,* he mentions Catullus as manifesting towards Lesbia such a temper of incompatibility as a man frequently exhibits towards himself, and translates the *Odi et amo* epigram in illustration:

> " I *hate, and yet I love thee too;*
> H*ow can that be? I know not how;*
> O*nly that so it is I know;*
> A*nd feel with torment that 'tis so.*"

Cowley understood Catullus in this matter badly; but his translation of the *Acme and Septimius* ode [236] seems to have been the first really intelligent and sympathetic English version of that beautiful lyric:

" Whilst on Septimius' panting breast
(Meaning nothing less than rest)
Acme lean'd her loving head,
Thus the pleas'd Septimius said:
' My dearest Acme, if I be
Once alive, and love not thee
With a passion far above
All that e'er was called love;
In a Libyan desert may
I become some lion's prey;
Let him, Acme, let him tear
My breast, when Acme is not there.'
The god of love, who stood to hear him,
(The god of love was always near him)
Pleased and tickled with the sound,
Sneezed aloud, and all around
The little Loves, that waited by,
Bowed, and blest the augury.
Acme, enflamed with what he said,
Reared her gently-bending head;
And, her purple mouth with joy
Stretching to the delicious boy,
Twice (and twice could scarce suffice)
She kist his drunken rolling eyes.
' My little life, my all!' (said she)
' So may we ever servants be
To this best god, and ne'er retain
Our hated liberty again!
So may thy passion last for me,

As *I a passion have for thee,*
Greater and fiercer much than can
Be conceived by thee a man!

.   .   .   .   .   .

Into my marrow is it gone,
Fixt and settled in the bone;
It reigns not only in my heart,
But runs, like life, through every part.'
She spoke; the god of love aloud
Sneezed again; and all the crowd
Of little Loves, that waited by,
Bowed, and blest the augury.
This good omen thus from Heaven
Like a happy signal given,   .
Their loves and lives (all four) embrace,
And hand in hand run all the race."

To this period also belongs Tom Brown's famous epigram, which through Martial goes back to Catullus: [237]

" *I do not love thee, Dr. Fell:*
The reason why I cannot tell:
But this alone I know full well,
I do not love thee, Dr. Fell."

But the seventeenth-century poet who drank deepest at the fount of Catullus was Robert Herrick, whose *Hesperides* mark " the su-

preme achievement of Renaissance song." [238]
Through Ben Jonson his classicism goes back
especially to Catullus, Horace and the Alexandrians. Lowell calls him " the most Catullian of poets since Catullus." [239] In his
spontaneity, his mastery of a wide range of
metrical forms, as well as of poetic types,
and his lyrical intensity he has caught the
spirit of his master; and though, to quote
Mr. Moorman once more, " he lacks the
passion of the Veronese lyrist," " he rivals
him in the terse precision of his style." The
ode, the epigram, and the *epithalamium* all
come in for their share of imitation. The
Vivamus, mea Lesbia well maintains in Herrick its claim to be the most popular of the
Catullian lyrics; for its more or less direct
influence can be traced in at least a half
dozen different products of Herrick's pen.
To Anthea he writes:

" *Give me a kiss, and to that kiss a score:*
Then to that twenty add a hundred more:
A thousand to that hundred: so kiss on,
To make the thousand up a million.
Treble that million, and when that is done
Let's kiss afresh, as when we first begun."

[178]

In the spirit of Catullus, if not in his language, is the last stanza of *Corinna's going a-Maying*, where he exhorts:

" *Come, let us go while we are in our prime;*
  And take the harmless folly of the time.
    We shall grow old apace, and die
    Before we know our liberty.
    Our life is short, and our days run
    As fast away as does the sun."

Lesbia's *Sparrow* is recalled in a little elegy, in which we read:

" *Phil, the late dead, the late dead dear,*
  O! may no eye distil a tear
  For you once lost, who weep not here!
  Had Lesbia, too-too kind, but known
  This sparrow, she had scorned her own:
  And for this dead which under lies
  Wept out her heart, as well as eyes."

Lesbia was dearer to Catullus than his very eyes; [240] Herrick, in the favorite lyric beginning:

    " *Bid me to live, and I will live,*"

concludes thus:

    " *Thou art my life, my love, my heart,*
      The very eyes of me:

> And hast command of every part
> To live and die for thee."

The joy expressed by Catullus in his return to Sirmio is reproduced in *The Plaudite*, or *End of Life*:

> " If *after rude and boisterous seas,*
> My *wearied pinnace here finds ease:*
> If *so it be I've gained the shore*
> With *safety of a faithful oar:*
> If *having run my barque on ground,*
> Ye *see the aged vessel crowned;*
> What's *to be done? but on the sands*
> Ye *dance and sing and now clap hands.*"

The napkin thief is paralleled by " Shark "; for after he has dined with you,

> " *if the servants search, they may descry*
> In *his wide codpeece, dinner being done,*
> Two *napkins crammed up and a silver spoon.*"

Suffenus, blind to his own weaknesses, is mirrored in this little epigram:

> " Other *men's sins we ever bear in mind;*
> None *sees the fardell of his faults behind,*"

a picture which Samuel Rowland had already painted in his satires with more detail. When

in Bacchanalian mood, Herrick calls forth a
succession of the poetic worthies of antiquity
to be toasted, and in due time comes to this
stanza:

> " *Then this immensive cup*
> *Of aromatic wine,*
> *Catullus, I quaff up*
> *To that terse muse of thine.*"

In the same poem he catches up the little
conceit of Catullus about his Lesbian per-
fume: [241]

> " *and suppose,*
> *Made he the pledge, he'd think*
> *The world had all one nose.*"

An elaboration of Catullus' theme, ' Venus
delights in loquacious prattle,' [242] is given in
Lips Tongueless:

> " *For my part, I never care*
> *For those lips that tongue-tied are:*
> *Tell-tales I would have them be*
> *Of my mistress and of me.*"

The fate of bad poetry humorously suggested
by Catullus [243] is twice referred to by Herrick,
in little addresses *To His Book:*

" Have *I not blest thee? Then go forth, nor fear*
  Or spice, or fish, or fire, or close-stools here; "

and again:

> " Lest, rapt from hence, I see thee lie
>   Torn for the use of pastery:
>   Or see the injured leaves serve well,
>   To make loose gowns for mackerel."

As Catullus did honor to his deceased brother
at the tomb in the far-away Troad,[244] so did
Herrick honor his father in the poem addressed
*To the Reverend Shade of his Religious
Father,* expressing regret at his delay in com-
ing, because of not knowing where to go:

" That for seven lusters I did never come
  To do the rites to thy religious tomb;

  .   .   .   .   .   .

  But now 'tis known, behold, behold I bring
  Unto thy ghost th' effused offering."

Perhaps his " religious father " would have
chided the son a little for certain lingering
signs of worldliness in his poetry. Catullus
could not outdo Herrick in the blunt realism
of his epigrams, some of which remind the
reader strikingly of the older poet; and often

enough in Herrick there are verses that enter
into the realm of the *Ipsithilla* type. But the
poet recognized that the proper time to read
much of his verse was when the revel was on,
or at least the spirit of mystery in the air:

> *"When laurel spirts i'th'fire, and when the hearth*
> *Smiles to itself, and gilds the roof with mirth;*
> *When up the thyrse is rais'd, and when the sound*
> *Of sacred orgies flies, around, around,"*

that is, amid a Bacchanalian rout like that
described by Catullus in the passage which
Herrick here had in mind.[245]

Herrick's *epithalamia* breathe throughout
the inspiration of the Catullian models, and
frequently follow the thought closely. They
exhibit also the charming variety of lyrical
metric which Catullus had first employed in
Latin for the admiration of the following centuries. A few sample verses only can be
quoted here, first, from the *Epithalamy to
Sir Thomas Southwell and his Lady:*

> *"These precious, pearly, purling tears*
> *But spring from ceremonious fears.*
> *And 'tis but native shame*
> *That hides the loving flame,*

> And may a while control
> The soft and am'rous soul;
> But yet love's fire will waste
> Such bashfulness at last.
> Then away; come, Hymen, guide
> To the bed the bashful bride.
>
> .   .   .   .   .
>
> And now the yellow veil at last
> Over her fragrant cheek is cast.
> Now seems she to express
> A bashful willingness:
> Showing a heart consenting,
> As with a will repenting."

More elaborately dainty is the chivalry and imagination of the *Epithalamy of Sir Clipseby Crew and his Lady.* One of its best stanzas follows:

" What's that we see from far? the spring of day
  Bloom'd from the east, or faint enjewelled May
    Blown out of April, or some new
    Star filled with glory to our view,
        Reaching at heaven,
    To add a nobler planet to the seven?
      Say, or do we not descry
  Some goddess in a cloud of tiffany
        To move, or rather the
      Emergent Venus from the sea? "

We have seen that the remarkable galaxy of English Renaissance lyrists rushed with enthusiasm into the new world of classical models and eagerly studied and imitated Catullus and his countrymen. In so doing they laid deep the foundation of all succeeding English poetry. In the sixteenth century the tone had been rather that of chivalrous idealism, following the lead of Petrarch. In the seventeenth century the directness and simplicity of the classic spirit re-asserted itself, and the movement was rather towards a realism manifested either in the amorous ecstacy or even the startling coarseness which reached a climax in Herrick. With Milton and Dryden, and their most important successors in the English poetry of the eighteenth century, literature reached a somewhat more sophisticated, or, as it has been termed, a "cosmopolitan" stage; and the prevailing feeling, for the time-being, was rather for polish than for passion. Poetry had become a genteel art, and the man of letters felt a new importance in the national life. Milton was an eminent classical scholar, who wrote good Latin prose and verse. But he wrote little lyric poetry except the paraphrases of the

[185]

Psalms. The temper of Catullus and that of the creator of *Paradise Lost* have little in common. That Milton and the other great masters of epic, didactic, satiric, or philosophic poetry in the seventeenth and eighteenth centuries were indebted in no small degree for poetic diction, form and figure to the Roman lyrist may well be assumed; but of course we should not expect to find in their major works such frequent allusions to, or imitations of, him as are scattered freely through the Renaissance singers of the preceding generations. That Milton, however, knew his Catullus is clear from his little Latin epigram on his famous antagonist, Salmasius, in the style of a learned Cantabrigian, beginning:

" Gaudete scombri, et quidquid est piscium salo,"

a verse in which reference is made to at least two of Catullus' poems.[246] He also employs the Catullian hendecasyllables in his Latin strophic poem addressed to John Rouse. Possibly such occasional reminiscences as that in the line,

" *Cheer'd with the grateful smell, old ocean smiles,*" [247]

[186]

indicate traces of Catullus' " little epic " in
the mind of the great author of the greatest
English epic.

Among the Queen Anne poets, Dean Swift
betrays every now and then his familiarity
with Catullus. In *Cadenus and Vanessa* he
is doubtless thinking of the Catullian message
to Caecilius,[248] as he writes:

> " *Cadenus many things had writ:*
> *Vanessa much esteem'd his wit,*
> *And call'd for his poetic works:*
> *Meantime the boy in secret lurks;*
> *And, while the book was in her hand,*
> *The urchin from his private stand*
> *Took aim, and shot with all his strength*
> *A dart of such prodigious length,*
> *It pierc'd the feeble volume through*
> *And deep transfix'd her bosom too.*
> *Some lines, more moving than the rest,*
> *Stuck to the point that pierc'd her breast,*
> *And, borne directly to the heart,*
> *With pains unknown increased her smart.*"

It is the Catullian joke on the effect of stupid
poetry [249] which Swift repeats in his *On Burning a Dull Poem:*

[187]

" *The cold conceits, the chilling thoughts,*
  Went down like stupefying draughts:
  I found my head began to swim,
  A numbness crept through every limb."

And probably the erratic Dean had in mind
Catullus' unsavory address to Rufus [250] when
he stooped to pen *The Problem,* about Lord
Berkeley. Why, of all the compositions of
the Roman writer he translated but one, it
would be hard to tell. He made various complete versions from Horace; but the only one
from Catullus seems to be this rendering: [251]

" *Lesbia forever on me rails.*
  To talk of me she never fails.
  Now, hang me, but for all her art,
  I find that I have gained her heart.
  My proof is this: I plainly see
  The case is just the same with me;
  I curse her every hour sincerely,
  Yet, hang me, but I love her dearly."

An important era of translation from the
Greek and Latin classics, indeed, had opened
in the later years of the seventeenth century,
and was continued with much vigor during
the next generations. The names of Dryden,

Creech, Pope, Rowe, West, and others of this group, suggest at once serious endeavor to present the English public with worthy versions of many of the leading classical authors. Virgil, Horace, Ovid, Juvenal, Lucretius, Claudian, and others of the Latin poets, rather than Catullus, seem to have appealed first to the more critical and less impassioned writers of this age. Pope, for example, made no Catullus versions; but he was familiar with the author, and included him in the list of the only eight " unexceptionally excellent " Roman poets. The Latin motto which he chose to prefix to his " letters " is the couplet,[252] neatly rendered by Cranstoun:

" When fond regret broods o'er old loves anew,
  And o'er lost friendship sheds the bitter tear."

In a letter to Steele he refers to Catullus' use of diminutives to express " endearment and concern," " the utmost love and tenderness." In a letter to Cromwell he asks, " Who besides Catullus and Voiture can write agreeably on trifles? " To write agreeably on trifles was not exactly Pope's long suit! Yet in the one poem in which he undertook to elaborate a trifle he won his greatest fame; and, curiously enough, the idea of that poem, *The Rape of the Lock,* in its ultimate analysis, was borrowed from Catullus. This appears in the lines: [253]

"A *sudden star, it shot through liquid air,*
And drew behind a radiant trail of hair.
Not Berenice's locks first rose so bright,[254]
The heav'ns bespangling with dishevelled light.
The sylphs behold it kindling as it flies,
And pleased pursue its progress through the skies.
. . . .
Then cease, bright nymph! to mourn the ravished
*   hair,*
Which adds new glory to the shining sphere!"

Another passage, at the end of Canto III,[255] derives from another part of the same elegy:

"*What time would spare, from steel receives its*
*   date,*
And monuments, like men, submit to fate!
Steel could the labor of the gods destroy,
And strike to dust th' imperial tow'rs of Troy;
Steel could the works of mortal pride confound,
And hew triumphal arches to the ground.
What wonder then, fair nymph! thy hairs should
*   feel*
The conqu'ring force of unresisted steel?"

[190]

No complete translation of Catullus appeared in English until later in the eighteenth century. Partial translations, or versions, of one or another single poem were common. Perhaps the next separate booklet of this kind after the *Phasellus ille* of 1579, already referred to, was *The Adventures of Catullus and History of his Amours with Lesbia* (London, 1707), from which Martin [256] quotes the following of the last verses of Catullus' No. 31:

" *Rejoice, ye waters of the Lake de Gard,*
  And let an universal mirth be heard;
  Laugh, till your stock of laughter's wholly spent,
  And your whole magazine of merriment."

Whether Ambrose Phillips' version is taken direct from Catullus, No. 51, or from Sappho is perhaps uncertain; it may be that he used both, to contrive the verses beginning:

  " *Blest as the immortal gods is he,*
    The youth who fondly sits by thee,
    And hears and sees thee all the while
    Softly speak and sweetly smile." [257]

A very neat song, reminding us of poems of Martial and Catullus on counting kisses, was written by Sir Charles Hanbury Williams.

[191]

The second stanza includes the Catullian enumeration: [258]

> " Count how many stars are in heaven,
>   Go reckon the sands on the shore,
> And when so many kisses you've given,
>   I still shall be asking for more."

But the temper of the poets of the later eighteenth century was not, as a rule, that of Catullus. Cowper and Gray made a few versions from the classics, but not from Catullus. The verses On the Death of Mrs. Throckmorton's Bullfinch are a far cry from Lesbia's Sparrow. Shenstone's The Dying Kid is a little nearer the spirit of Catullus' poem. When Thomson in Liberty writes: [259]

> " See where it runs from the deep-loaded plains
>   Of Mauritania to the Libyan sands,
> Where Ammon lifts amid the torrid waste
>   A verdant isle, with shade and fountain fresh,"

he may be reminiscent of Catullus.

The only poet of the dying eighteenth century who has the true Catullian mood is Burns. The two men were of like temperaments,[260] though of decidedly different stations in life; and certainly their poetry has many striking thoughts in common. It would be rash to assert that the many parallels which have been pointed out are all due to an acquaintance with Catullus on the part of Burns; but it is at least quite possible that some of the most evident similarities in Burns directly or indirectly derive from the Roman poet. The beautiful figure of the flower crushed by the passing plow,[261] which Catullus uses twice, is the pervading idea of *To a Mountain Daisy:*

> " *Thou lifts thy unassuming head*
>   *In humble guise;*
> *But now the share uptears thy bed,*
>   *And low thou lies!*
>
> *Such is the fate of artless maid,*
> *Sweet flow'ret of the rural shade!*
> *By love's simplicity betray'd,*
>   *And guileless trust;*
> *Till she, like thee, all soil'd, is laid*
>   *Low i' the dust.*"

When Burns sings:

> " *O wad some power the giftie gie us*
> *To see oursels as ithers see us,*"

we recall the moral at the end of the Suffenus poem of Catullus.[262] Like the Roman poet, Burns knew the

" *Cheerless night that knows no morrow*," [263]

and in the following lines, he expressed a reminiscent sadness, characteristic of Catullus:

" *Farewell, hours that late did measure*
Sunshine days of joy and pleasure." [264]

And even if we dare do no more, it is at least interesting to compare Catullus' exclamation over the rapture of his meeting with Lesbia at the house of Allius,[265] with the following lines:

" O *May, thy morn was ne'er sae sweet*
As *the mirk night o' December!*
F*or sparkling was the rosy wine,*
And *private was the chamber,*
And *dear was she I dare na name,*
But *I will ay remember.*"

It is Arthur Symons [266] who says that " after Burns, though no one could sing like him, no one has returned to the delusion that the poet need not be a singer." It is attributable to the lack of an inspired emotion in so many of the greater poets of the eighteenth century that so little, relatively, of Catullus' influence appears in them. Dryden, Pope, Addison and Johnson were great critics, great rhymesters, great satirists, perhaps great moralists; they can hardly be known as great interpreters of the human heart. They were good classical scholars in their often rather pedantic way. Richard Steele, after a night spent in conversation with Addison, remarks that he " had had the pleasure of conversing with an intimate acquaintance of Terence and Catullus." Even Collins and Gray wrote good Latin verse. But in the nineteenth century, as Mr. Chislett remarks, there came " an almost Renaissance revival of scholarship," which was " tempered with a finer critical sense; with a surer understanding of ancient life and literature; with a concern with spirit as much as letter." Or, as Professor Shorey has put it: [267] " the vision of antiquity " to the nineteenth century is " the re-capture of something of that first careless Renaissance rapture tempered by a finer historical sense, controlled by a more critical scholarship." And, he continues, it is because of the early acquaintance with the classics on the part of those who won great repute down through the history of English poesy to the present that "no other European literature is so rich in spontaneous and luxuriant classical imagery, or in the exquisite reminiscence and adaptation of classic phrase." Byron, Shelley,[268] Browning, Swinburne, Arnold and Tennyson drew heavily on the inspiration of the classics, to say nothing of the Coleridges, of Keats, Wordsworth and many lesser lights.

In this new combination of sound scholarship and sympathetic imagination it is not strange that Catullus has returned to a more general and a deeper appreciation than ever, and has exerted a more profound influence on English poetry, that imitations and translations of the Roman lyrist abound, and that critical estimates of his merit are numerous and high. Coleridge in his *Biographia Literaria* tells how his schoolmaster "habituated" him to read Catullus and some other early Latin poets, to compare them with the Augustan poets, "and on grounds of plain sense and universal logic to see and assert the superiority of the former in the truth and nativeness both of their thoughts and diction." Swinburne considered Catullus' mastery of

verse-form "complete," and looked upon him
as a "literary god." Morris includes him
among the "real ancient imaginative" poets.
Tennyson made him a vital factor in his own
life and work. "I love Catullus," he said,[269]
"for his perfection in form and for his tenderness, the tenderest of Roman poets," quoting
to Thackeray at a dinner party, as illustrating
this, the same couplet which Pope had pre-
fixed to his *Letters*. And when he returned
from a trip to Italy, the words that came to
his lips on entering his own home [270] were the
words of Catullus — that sigh of satisfaction
uttered by the weary wanderer on reaching
his own fireside:

"O quid solutis est beatius curis?" [271]

Martin has rendered them thus:

" O *what more sweet than when, from care set free,*
The spirit lays its burden down, and we,
With distant travel spent, come home and spread
Our limbs to rest along the wished-for bed:
This, this alone repays such toils as these!"

Byron, whose own nature was not so unlike
that of Catullus, has various references to the
Roman poet in his letters and notes, and in

certain passages of *Don Juan, The Age of Bronze,* and elsewhere. Similarities like that in the opening lines of *The Giaour:*

> " There, mildly dimpling, Ocean's cheek
> Reflects the tints of many a peak
> Caught by the laughing tides that lave
> These Edens of the eastern wave," [272]

or in the lines:

> " But mine was like the lava flood
> That boils in Aetna's breast of flame," [273]

need not be emphasized. When he writes to Thomas Moore:

> " But tomorrow at four we will both play the Scurra,
> And you'll be Catullus, the Regent Mamurra,"

he showed a keen appreciation of Catullus' wit, which Leigh Hunt, to whom reference is here made, little enjoyed. Catullus he calls a " scholar of love," and defends his *Attis* from the absurd charge of " licentiousness." The poem, *To Lesbia,* reflects the spirit of more than one of Catullus' lyrics. Byron, however, chose for translation or paraphrase

the 3d, 48th and 51st of Catullus' lyrics,
which open respectively as follows:

" Ye *Cupids, droop each little head,*
Nor let your wings with joy be spread.
My Lesbia's favorite bird is dead,
Whom dearer than her eyes she lov'd; "

" Oh! *might I kiss those eyes of fire,*
A million scarce would quench desire;
Still would I steep my lips in bliss,
And dwell an age on every kiss; "

" Equal *to Jove that youth must be —*
Greater than Jove he seems to me —
Who, free from Jealousy's alarms,
Securely views thy matchless charms."

Versions of certain favorite poems are often
met with in leading writers of this period.
Leigh Hunt begins thus to render the joy of
Catullus upon returning to Sirmio:

" O *best of all the scatter'd spots that lie*
In sea or lake, — apple of landscape's eye, —
How gladly do I drop within thy nest,
With what a sigh of full contented rest,
Scarce able to believe my journey o'er,
And that these eyes behold thee safe once more! "

[199]

Hunt has also a version of the pathetic appeal
to Cornificius,[274] beginning:

> " Sick, Cornificius, is thy friend,
>   Sick to the heart; and sees no end
>   Of wretched thoughts, that, gathering fast,
>   Threaten to wear him out at last."

He also made a translation of the *Acme and
Septimius,* as did Elton. Elton tried his hand
also on the *Sirmio* poem, and so did Moore.
Calverley did it in sonnet form:

> " Gem of all isthmuses and isles that lie,
>   Fresh or salt water's children, in clear lake
> Or ampler ocean: with what joy do I
>   Approach thee, Sirmio! Oh! am I awake,
> Or dream that once again mine eye beholds
> Thee, and has looked its last on Thracian wolds?
>   Sweetest of sweets that pastime seems,
> When the mind drops her burden: when — the
>   pain
> Of travel past — our own cot we regain,
>   And nestle on the pillow of our dreams!
> 'Tis this one thought that cheers us as we roam.
>   Hail! O fair Sirmio! Joy, thy lord is here!
>   Joy, too, ye waters of the Golden Mere!
> And ring out, all ye laughter-peals of home! "

Hartley Coleridge based a dainty little poem on the *Sparrow* of Catullus, the first part of which runs as follows:

> " Little sparrow, pretty sparrow,
>   Darling of my ' winsome marrow,'
>   Plaything, playmate, what you will,
>   Tiny love, or naughty Phil,
>   Tempted, teased, to peck and hop
>   On her slender finger top,
>   Free to nuzzle and to rest
>   In the sweet valley of her breast;
> Her wee, wee comfort in her sorrow's wane,
> When sinks to sleep the fever of her pain."

In mourning the death of the sparrow, he is even nearer the original:

> " Weep and wail, ye Cupids all,
>   That are pretty and but small;
>
>   .   .   .   .   .   .
>
>   He is dead, the pretty sparrow,
>   Darling of my ' winsome marrow,'
>
>   .   .   .   .   .   .
>
>   Not a moment would he quit her,
>   Hopping hither, flitting thither,
>
>   .   .   .   .   .   .
>
>   Now the dark way he is wending,
>   Whence, they say, is no ascending.
>
>   .   .   .   .   .   .

Alas! poor bird — oh deed of sorrow!
My sweet one's eyes, with tears so salt
Are red and swollen; 'tis all thy fault."

In his critical essay on *The Poems of Catullus*, Landor modestly offers a number of sympathetic versions: passages in the *Peleus and Thetis*, part of the first renunciation of Lesbia, the humorous incident with Varus' mistress, the jesting invitation of Fabullus to dinner, the contemptuous estimate of Suffenus the poetaster, Nos. 87 and 75 together (as they were formerly printed in many editions), the *Odi et amo*, the epigram on Caesar, and parts of others. Only examples of these can be quoted:

" I *love and hate. Ah! never ask why so!*
I *hate and love. . . . and that is all I know.*
I *see 'tis folly, but I feel 'tis woe."* [275]

" I *care not, Caesar, what you are,*
Nor *know if ye be brown or fair."* [276]

" None *could ever say that she,*
Lesbia! *was so loved by me.*
Never *all the world around*
Faith *so true as mine was found.*
If *no longer it endures*
(Would *it did!) the fault is yours.*

I *can never think again*
W*ell of you: I try in vain.*
B*ut . . be false . . do what you will. —*
L*esbia! I must love you still."* 277

"E*gnatius has fine teeth, and those*
E*ternally Egnatius shows.*
S*ome criminal is being tried*
F*or murder; and they open wide;*
A *widow wails her only son;*
W*idow and him they open on.*
'T*is a disease, I'm very sure,*
A*nd wish 'twere such as you could cure,*
M*y good Egnatius! for what's half*
S*o silly as a silly laugh?"* 278

"W*ith me, Fabullus, you shall dine,*
    A*nd gaudily, I promise you,*
I*f you will only bring the wine,*
    T*he dinner, and some beauty too."* 279

The story of Varus' mistress he tells most
happily. At length, be it remembered, the
girl asked Catullus to loan her six or eight
litter-bearers:

" ' W*hy, six or eight of them or so,'*
    S*aid I, determined to be grand,*
 ' M*y fortune is not quite so low,*
    B*ut these are still at my command.'*

'*You'll send them!*' '*Willingly!*' *I told her,*
  Altho' I had not here or there
One who could carry on his shoulder
  The leg of an old broken chair.
'*Catullus! what a charming hap is*
  Our meeting in this sort of way!
I would be carried to Serapis
  Tomorrow.' '*Stay, fair lady, stay!*
You overvalue my intention.
  Yes, there are *eight. . . there may be nine. . .*
I merely had forgot to mention
  That they are Cinna's and not mine.'"

Severe critic as he is, Landor has words of
superlative praise for Catullus, that " bard of
Sirmio " on whom,

> "*Thalia's son,*
> *Such stains there are as when a Grace*
> *Sprinkles another's laughing face*
> *With nectar, and runs on.*"

" No human works are so perfect as some
of his;" in comparison with Horace, though
Horace " has much," " Catullus has greatly
more than he;" the Ariadne episode is a case
where " the pathetic is the very summit of
sublimity;" and, after many frank criticisms
of certain faults, appears this characteristic

peroration: "They who have listened, patiently and supinely, to the catarrhal songsters of goose-grazed commons, will be loth and ill-fitted to mount up with Catullus to the highest steeps in the forests of Ida, and will shudder at the music of the Corybantes in the temple of the Great Mother of the Gods."

The amusing parody on *Acme and Septimius*,[280] made by J. Hookham Frere, who was well acquainted with official life, should not be forgotten. A stanza will give its flavor:

" *Fox, with Tooke to grace his side,*
  Thus addressed his blooming bride —
  ' Sweet! should I e'er, in power or place,
  Another citizen embrace;
  Should e'er my eyes delight to look
  On aught alive, save John Horne Tooke,
  Doom me to ridicule and ruin
  In the coarse hug of Indian Bruin! '
    He spoke; and to the left and right,
    Norfolk hiccupped with delight."

That political satire could adopt this form is sufficient indication how thoroughly familiar educated English circles at the end of the eighteenth century were with Catullus. But it was not always in that mood that Frere attacked the problem of translation. For his versions of other Catullian poems show delicate appreciation of the mood of the author and a mastery of English poetical expression, worthy of the original. The last stanza, for example, of the *epithalamium* of Manlius and Vinia, as he phrases it, reads:

> "*With laughing eyes and dewy lip,*
>   *Pouting like the purple tip*
>   *That points the rose's bud;*
>   *While mingled with the mother's grace,*
>   *Strangers shall recognize the trace*
>   *That marks the Manlian blood;* "

and the concluding lines of his rendering of Catullus' experience with Varus' mistress catch the spirit of Catullus himself:

> "*But you have caught the general vice*
>   *Of being too correct and nice,*
>   *Over curious and precise;*
>   *And seizing with precipitation*
>   *The slight neglects of conversation.*"

Wide is the gulf separating the humorous verses of Frere from the *Ave atque Vale* of Swinburne, which, with all of its alien wealth of imagination and beauty of imagery, none

the less took its inspiration from the same
noble poem of Catullus [281] that meant so much
to Tennyson. Opening with the question:

" *Shall I strew on thee rose or rue or laurel,*
  Brother, on this that was the veil of thee? "

he recalls the Catullian rovings, —

" *Thine ears knew all the wandering watery sighs*
  Where the sea sobs round Lesbian promontories,
  The barren kiss of piteous wave to wave
  That knows not where is that Leucadian grave
  Which hides too deep the supreme head of song."

He, too, would make his offering to the
memory of the dead:

" *For thee, O now a silent soul, my brother,*
  Take at my hands this garland, and farewell."

How highly Swinburne esteemed Catullus may
be gathered from his Latin poem *Ad Catullum*,
from his imitation of the Catullian meters,
and from his admission that when we under-
take to imitate the Roman poet, he " makes
mouths at our speech."

Grant Allen has published a metrical translation of the *Attis* in a special edition. A translation of the *Lock of Berenice* has been made

by Tytler. George Moore and Arthur Symons have prepared versions of Catullus. Others who have successfully caught the meaning of Catullus and given us worthy English renderings of individual poems are Richard Jebb, Tyrrell, Davies, Aubrey Beardsley, and Hummel and Brodribb (whose imitation of the Arrius epigram is worth quoting):

" Whenever 'Arry tried to sound
 An H, his care was unavailing;
He always spoke of 'orse and 'ound,
 And all his kinsfolk had that failing.
Peace to our ears. He went from home;
 But tidings came that grieved us bitterly —
That 'Arry, while he stayed at Rome,
 Enjoyed his 'oliday in Hitaly."

Baron Thurlow did the *Ariadne* in 1814.

We have already spoken of Tennyson's enthusiasm for Catullus. He disagreed, to be sure, with him in the notion that it made no difference if a poet's verses were " impure, provided his life be pure." For, he added, " his verses fly much further than he does." But, he went on: " I have always admired him: ' Acme and Septimius ' is lovely. Then he has very pretty metres. ' Collis O Heliconii ' is in a beautiful metre. I wrote a great part of my ' Jubilee Ode ' in it." [282] Such intense devotion to Catullus and other ancient writers produced a profound effect on the work of this popular modern English poet. It resulted in a " reproduction of the very soul " of Catullus and of other Greek and Roman poets, and brought forth many a thought that " was nourished on the literature and philosophy of Greece and Rome." [283] " Tennyson need not fear comparison with the scholarly poets who preceded him. . . . Not one of them, not even rare Ben himself, was more thoroughly imbued with the spirit of classical antiquity than the author of the *Lotos Eaters*." [284] And so we can hardly stop to enumerate all the references and allusions to Catullus in Tennyson, many of which are palpable enough, while others are doubtless more elusive. When, in *Edwin Morris,* he addresses him thus:

> " *Shall not Love to me,*
> A*s in the Latin song I learnt at school,*
> S*neeze out a full God-bless-you right and left,*"

we know at once that Tennyson is thinking of the *Acme and Septimius*. The last stanza of *Eleänore* is surely reminiscent of the Sapphic strains of Catullus: [285]

> " I *watch thy grace; and in its place*
> My *heart a charmed slumber keeps,*
>   While *I muse upon thy face;*
> And *a languid fire creeps*
>   Through *my veins to all my frame,*
> Dissolvingly *and slowly. Soon*
>   From *thy rose-red lips* MY *name*
> Floweth; *and then, as in a swoon,*
>   With *dinning sound my ears are rife,*
>   My *tremulous tongue faltereth,*
> I *lose my colour, I lose my breath,*
> I *drink the cup of a costly death,*
> Brimm'd *with delirious draughts of warmest life.*"

The *Peleus and Thetis* may have suggested lines in the *Guinevere* [286] and also in *Lancelot and Elaine,*[287] while very possibly the " wild team " in *Tithonus* [288] owes much to the description of the sunrise in Catullus' *Attis.* The form of expression in the verses,[289]

> " And *come, whatever loves to weep,*
>   And *hear the ritual of the dead,*"

was not improbably suggested by a favorite manner of Catullus. The popular ode on the

[210]

death of the pet sparrow Tennyson has even more surely, if it were possible, immortalized by his expression:

" *And you, that wear a wreath of sweeter bay,*
  Catullus, whose dead songster never dies." [290]

Professor Mustard cites other parallels. Let us here refer to but one other poem of Catullus, his elegy at the tomb of his brother.[291] It is evidently of this that Tennyson was thinking when, in the *In Memoriam,*[292] he wrote:

" I *hear it now, and o'er and o'er,*
   Eternal greetings to the dead;
   And ' Ave, Ave, Ave,' said,
 ' *Adieu, adieu,' for evermore.*"

And it is the same little elegy of which the modern poet uses this superlative language: " Nor can any modern elegy, so long as men retain the least hope in the after-life of those whom they have loved, equal in pathos the desolation of that everlasting farewell, ' Atque in perpetuum, frater, ave atque vale.' " This is the text and title of one of the best known of Tennyson's shorter poems. When in 1880 his physician ordered him to travel, he visited Munich, the Tyrol and northern Italy, and

with peculiar delight hunted up the old country place of Catullus on the Lago di Garda.
" Over Sirmio, the peninsula of Catullus,"
writes his son,[293] " we roamed all day. My
father liked this, I think, the best of anything we had seen on our tour: its olives, its
old ruins, and its greensward stretching down
to the blue lake with the mountains beyond.
Here he made his ' Frater, Ave atque Vale ' " :

" R*ow us out from Desenzano, to your Sirmione
row!*
So *they row'd, and then we landed — O venusta
Sirmio!*
T*here to me thro' all the grove of olives in the
summer glow,*
T*here beneath the Roman ruin where the purple
flowers grow,*
C*ame that ' Ave atque Vale' of the poet's hope-
less woe,*
T*enderest of Roman poets nineteen hundred
years ago,*
' F*rater, Ave atque Vale' — as we wandered to
and fro*
G*azing at the Lydian laughter of the Garda
lake below,*
S*weet Catullus' all-but-island, olive-silvery Sir-
mio!* " [294]

How Catullus himself would have gone into raptures over that wonderful picture-word, " olive-silvery," made in his own mold! And how he would have loved the sympathetic soul of his brother poet after nineteen hundred years!

Tennyson, as we know, was charmed with the Catullian meters, and imitated several of the most characteristic ones. The favorite Hendecasyllables are illustrated in these verses:

" Look, I come to the test, a tiny poem
All composed in a metre of Catullus."

The Glyconics of the *Jubilee Ode* run like this:

" You then joyfully, all of you,
Set the mountain aflame tonight,
Shoot yourselves to the firmament," etc.

His fondness for Trochaics may very probably have been fostered by the Phalæcians of Catullus. His Leonine Elegiacs began:

" Low-flowing breezes are roaming the broad
valley dimm'd in the gloaming."

Even the wild and uncontrollable Galliambics of the *Attis* he yoked and drove through his *Boädicëa,* one line of which will suffice:

" *These have told us all their anger in miraculous utterances.*"

George Meredith too in his *Phaëthon* tried the Galliambics. Indeed, the direct effect of Catullus' meters on English metric is not inconsiderable, though the indirect effect is much greater. Phalæcians, before Tennyson, had been written, for example, by Sir Philip Sidney and by Coleridge (*Catullian Hendecasyllables*); and Swinburne used them in his poem beginning:

" *In the month of the long decline of roses.*"

So did J. A. Symonds:

" O *the wonderful eyes of contadini!*
  O *the ring of their voices on the hill-sides!* "

Swinburne also tried his hand at Sapphics. Campion's contributions to metric were based on Catullus. And who shall say how much, more or less indirectly, a host of English poets, from Milton to Matthew Arnold, owe to the metrical forms and fashions of Catullus?

It is only in our own time that Robinson Ellis has ventured to translate the whole of the Catullus collection into English verse of the original meters, a remarkable exhibition of his mastery of his author and of both languages. Translation, however, of the whole *corpus* of Catullus into English verse has been successfully accomplished by several other writers, including Dr. John Nott, who published an anonymous edition in 1795, George Lamb in 1821, James Cranstoun in 1867, and Davies in 1879. Burton and Smithers produced a translation, part in prose and part in verse, in 1894. The Loeb library in recent years has given us the version of Cornish. Stuttaford published a prose translation in 1912. Theodore Martin's elegant renderings do not include all of the Catullus collection, but give us most of it that is worth while. Both Tremenheere and Macnaghten also have published some beautiful versions of many of the poems which reveal more particularly the life history of the poet. The general effect of making Catullus more accessible in English poetry will be, we hope, a great stimulus to literary culture and literary creation in the twentieth century.

The presence in Oxford of one of the best manuscripts of Catullus is, of course, partly responsible for the fact that the epoch-making critical edition and commentary of Ellis brought renown in Catullus scholarship to England. Munro's work, and that of various other English classical scholars, has greatly added to this fame. Nowhere is this poet more widely known, studied, and loved, than in England. Editions and translations of one or another poem or cycle of his poems are constantly being put forth. Indeed no better indication, perhaps, of the importance of Catullus to English culture can be pointed out than the list of books in the Catullus library of the British Museum, which includes nearly three hundred separate titles besides duplicates. The Museum has over a hundred separate editions of the poems in Latin, many editions of selections, translations into most of the European languages, including Greek, Hungarian, Polish, and Swedish, and scores of studies of the poet from every standpoint. This diffusion of knowledge of Catullus has accordingly made him almost a household word.

There is nothing provincial, moreover, as we have seen, about this perennial interest in Catullus. In America that interest seems to be growing rather than evincing any signs of a decline. Some of the most popular and generally used editions of the poet have been published in this country within recent years, and in the period between 1902 and 1915 three distinct translations of select poems of Catullus appeared, in Philadelphia, Boston, and Chicago respectively. Other original versions are included in Dole's *Anthology of Latin Poets*. So, although the active pursuit of tangibles in the ultra-modern life of America has too often crowded out the earnest study of the more enduring intangibles, it is not over-optimistic to cherish the hope that more and more in America too, as has been the case for so many centuries in England, there will develop an abiding eagerness to know both the " spirit and the content of ancient literature and life." [295] For, as Walter Pater has said, the classics come to us " out of the cool and quiet of other times, as the measure of what a long experience has shown will never displease us. And in the classical literatures of Greece and Rome, . . . the essentially classical element

[217]

is that quality of order in beauty, which they possess indeed in a preëminent degree." [296] Emotion never dies from the soul of mankind, and " Catullus' expression of emotion has the Greek qualities of definiteness, adequacy, point, and necessary limitation." [297]

VII. CONCLUSION

IT was Catullus who taught Europe, and America, how to sing tender songs of love, to phrase bitter words of hate; who "pointed the way to a more exact prosody and a richer versification;" [298] who showed us how to flash on the mental retina whole pictures in a single word; who left an imperishable imprint of a throbbing human heart which will always appeal to every other soul of man. He

"who loves the flame
That leaped within Catullus the divine," [299]

will agree with Macnaghten that "it is to Shakespeare and Catullus, above all others, that lovers will always turn, because they alone convince us that as they have written 'so should such things be.'" [300]

Among the shorter poems which are deathless and have constantly influenced the poets of all succeeding ages we must certainly recognize the tender verses on Lesbia's sparrow, the invitation to her to love devotedly while life lasts, the passionate demand for kisses without number, the greeting to his beloved Sirmio after long absence, the idyll of Acme and Septimius, the Sapphic adaptation of the old Greek ode of the love-lorn maiden to express his own enthrallment by his " Lesbia," the terrible discovery that her words might as well be written on wind and water, his agonizing prayer to the gods for help to shake off his love, the inimitable ' I love and I hate,' and the sad farewell at his brother's tomb. Of his longer poems the *Epithalamia* especially were responsible for a whole stream of verse flowing down the ages, while choice passages and similes from them have been imitated in various lands and tongues. He set the pace for epigram throughout the centuries.

The poetic qualities of beauty, simplicity, directness, sincerity and genuine emotion have appealed to his successors with a force unparalleled among classical writers. " In Catullus there is not the chivalry of love which characterizes the troubadours of Provence or the more idealistic treatment of passion in the *Minnelieder* of Germany. Catullus is at once more elemental, sensuous, and frank. So all the Hellenism in him — and it is only in part Alexandrine — is outweighed by that 'simplicité passionée' which so many of his critics have followed Fénelon in emphasizing." [301]

The lyric meters naturalized at Rome by Catullus were the basis of classical and medieval Latin lyric poetry; and it was he who popularized the elegiac distich and made it the vehicle for various other types of poetic expression besides the erotic elegy, as it remained for many centuries.

Even in other realms of art the influence of Catullus is felt. To be sure we may not chance to recall the *Peleus and Thetis* when in the National Gallery at London we gaze upon an Ariadne displaying all the opulence of Titian's coloring. But more and more, as our souls are prepared to receive such delicate messages, we may be able to detect, wafted to us on ethereal waves, the tender voice of the Roman singer of long ago.

NOTES AND BIBLIOGRAPHY

NOTES

All translations in single quotes in this book are those of K. P. H.

1. Cf. G. S. Gordon, *Eng. Lit. and the Classics*, Oxford, 1912, p. 155.   **1a.** 68. 20 ff.: Martin.
2. 68.15.   **3.** 17.   **4.** 67.   **5.** 1.   **5a.** 22.
6. 50: Martin.
7. Version by J. C. Rollo, of Glasgow University, quoted by Slater.
8. Cornish.   **9.** Martin.   **10.** 7 : Martin.
11. 5 : Tremenheere, p. 51.   **12.** 86 : Tremenheere.
13. 83 : Nott.   **14.** 76. 17 ff.   **15.** 70 : Cranstoun.   **16.** 72 : Nott.   **17.** 77.   **18.** 73: Cranstoun.
19. 85.   **20.** 76 : Cranstoun.   **21.** 101 : Slater.
22. 4.   **23.** 46.   **24.** 31.   **25.** 51A.
26. 53.   **27.** 11 : Tremenheere, p. 172.
28. 87 : Macnaghten.   **29.** Cf. Slater.   **30.** 34.
31. 31.   **32.** 2.   **33.** 109.   **34.** 101.
35. 1.   **36.** 9.   **37.** 35.   **38.** 58.
39. 65.   **40.** 95.   **41.** 96.   **42.** 102.
43. 49.   **44.** 50.   **45.** 61.   **46.** 38.
47. 6.   **48.** 13.   **49.** 14.   **50.** 36 and 95.
51. 44.   **52.** 17.   **53.** 26.   **54.** 10.
55. 84.   **56.** 7.   **57.** 17.   **58.** 61 : Cornish.
59. 64 : Martin.   **60.** 68 : Ellis.   **61.** 62: Martin.
62. F. P. Simpson, *Select Poems of Catullus*, London, 1880; Appendix II.
63. Cf. H. A. J. Munro, *Lucretius*, Cambridge, England; III. 57; also *Criticisms and Elucidations of Catullus*, Cambridge, England, 1878, p. 72.
64. J. W. Mackail, *The Progress of Poesy*, Oxford, 1906, p. 25.

NOTES

65. W. Y. Sellar, *Roman Poets of the Republic*, Oxford, 1889, p. 438.

66. Munro, *Criticisms and Elucidations*, p. 231.

67. Slater. **68.** Martin. **69.** Martin.

70. "Martial and the Satiric Epigram," in *Classical Philology*, xvii. 6 (1922).

71. 11. 4–5. **72.** 51. 5. **73.** Cf. Cat., 45. 10.

74. Cf. Cat., 51. 7 ff. **75.** Cf. Cat., 61. 33–35.

76. *Crit. & Eluc.*, p. 238. **77.** *Odes*, III. 9.

78. *Sat.*, I. 10. 19. **79.** Statius, *Silvae*, III. 4.

80. *Silvae*, IV. 9. **81.** Slater's version.

82. *Silvae*, II. 4. **83.** Slater. **84.** *Silvae*, II. 1: Slater. **85.** XIX. 40. **86.** 5.

87. Cf. Magnus, in *Jahresbericht für Altertumswissenschaft*, LI. ii. p. 240 (1887).

88. V. 24. 16. **89.** XVIII. 29. 21. **90.** 63. 21.

91. Cf., e.g., No. 5 with Tib., I. 1. 69–72.

92. E. K. Rand, in *Harvard Studies in Classical Philology*, xvii. 17 ff. (1906). **92a.** Martin.

93. Cf. Pliny, *Ep.*, I. 16. 5; also V. 3.

94. T. R. Glover, *Life and Letters in the Fourth Century*, Cambridge, England, 1901, p. 113.

95. XII. 83; versions by W. C. A. Ker, (*Martial, Epigrams*, with an English translation), in *The Loeb Classical Library*. 2 vols. New York, 1919–1920.

96. X. 78. 16. **97.** VII. 99. 6. **98.** IV. 14. 13.

99. XIV. 195. **100.** XIV. 77. **101.** I. 109. 1.

102. VII. 14. 3. **103.** I. 7. **104.** XI. 6. 14.

105. XII. 59. 1. **106.** VI. 34: from Cranstoun's *Catullus*. **107.** II. 86. 1–6.

108. See list in Schwabe's edition, pp. vii.–xvi.

109. *Silv.*, I. 2. 271–272 (Cranstoun); cf. Cat., 61. 221, ff.

110. *Epith. Pall. & Cel.* 124, ff.; cf. Cat., 61. 56, ff. (Cranstoun).

111. *Epith. Pall.* 31–33; cf. Cat., 61. 61, ff. (Cranstoun).

112. Claud., *Rapt. Pros.*, III. 407–411; cf. Cat., 64. 139, ff.

113. W. Y. Sellar, *Hor. & the Eleg. Poets*, Oxford, 1892, pp. 130, 197.

114. Intr., p. 23.

NOTES

115. B. Barwinski, in *Rheinisches Museum*, XLIII. 310–311 (1888).

116. J. E. Sandys, *A History of Class. Scholarship*, Cambridge, England, 1903; I. 603.

117. *Rhein. Mus.*, XLIII. p. 309.

118. Ellis: *Catullus in the XIVth Century*.

119. 70. 4.

120. Sonnet 177; Macgregor's translation (*Sonnets, Triumphs, and other Poems of Petrarch, translated by various hands*, London, 1893).

121. 7. 7–8.   **122.** *Sestina* 1; Macgregor.

123. Cat., 99. 3–4.   **124.** Cat., 86.   **125.** *Canz.*; Martin, p. 145.

126. Cat., 75; cf. Martin, p. 154.   **127.** *Or. Fur.*, 9. 435.

128. 18. 1060; Hoole's version; cf. Cat., 11. 22.

129. 62. 39, ff.   **130.** *Or. Fur.*, 1. 300; Hoole.

131. 14. 734; Hoole.   **132.** 7. 7–8.

133. Cat., 64. 269, ff.; cf. Ariosto: "Quod verni suol nel salso lido," etc.

134. Cat., 43. 1; cf. Ariosto: "il breve asciutto," etc.

135. 62. 39, ff.   **136.** 16. 99; Hoole.

137. *Tri. Cupid*, III. 159–163; Jerrold.

138. Cf. Schwabe, *Catullus*, p. xvii.

139. Foregoing versions by Richard Aldington, *Latin Poems of the Renaissance* (*The Egoist*), London, 1919.

140. F. J. Snell, *The Fourteenth Century*, New York, 1899, p. 157.

141. Snell, *ibid.*, p. 159.

142. Joseph Vianey, *Le Pétrarquisme en France au XVIe. Siècle*, Montpellier, 1909, p. 19.

143. Arthur Tilley, *The Literature of the French Renaissance*, Cambridge, England, 1904; 1, 73.

144. *Epigrammes* CCXV.   **145.** No. CCXXIV.

146. *E.g.*, *Epig.* XLIII; cf. Cat., 57.

147. Cum te rogabo ter tria basia, etc.

148. Cf. Cat., 7 and 48.   **149.** 51. 9–12.

150. Émile Faguet: *Seizième Siècle, Études Littéraires*, Paris, 1894, p. 319.

NOTES

151. Charles Marty-Laveaux, *Euvres en Rime de Ian Antoine de Baïf*, Paris, 1881, Vol. I., p. 48.

152. *Op. cit.*, p. 60.　　**153.** *Op. cit.*, p. 70.

154. *Op. cit.*, p. 73.　　**155.** A. Lang.

156. Cf. also No. 58.　　**157.** No. 46.　　**158.** Cat., 86.

159. Cat., 5.　　　　　**160.** Cf. Cat., 5 and 46.

161. *Carmina Burana*, Ed. by J. A. Schmeller, Breslau, 1904, p. 183.

162. *Op. cit.*, p. 195.　　**163.** *Op. cit.*, p. 167.

164. *Wine, Women, and Song*, London, 1907, p. 116.

165. 5.　　**166.** 92.　　**167.** Martin, p. 155.

168. G. Pellissier, *The Literary Movement in France during the Nineteenth Century*, New York, 1897.

169. Cat., 86.　　　　　**170.** Version by Martin, p. 144.

171. *Poems, translated, etc.*, by Frank Sewall, New York, 1892, p. 89.

172. Cat., 31. 1.　　　**173.** 4. 24.　　**174.** 58.

175. J. Robertson, *A Century of French Verse*, London, 1895, p. 14.

176. 5.　　**177.** Robertson, p. 100.　　**178.** 7. 8.

179. Cat., 68.　　**180.** Robertson, p. 113.　　**181.** Cat., 7.

182. Cat., 61. 78.　　**183.** Robertson, p. 195.

184. Cat., 63. 83.　　**185.** Robertson, p. 247.

186. Robertson, p. 115.

187. G. Otto Trevelyan, *The Life and Letters of Lord Macaulay*, New York, 1876; I. 410.

188. *Life;* II. 378.　　**189.** 8.　　**190.** 38.

191. 76.

192. Rev. Thomas Twining, *Recreations and Studies of a Country Clergyman of the Eighteenth Century*, London, 1882, p. 240.

193. Cat., 4.　　**194.** p. 26.

195. J. M. Berdan, *Early Tudor Poetry*, New York, 1920, pp. 261–262.

196. Ovid, *Her.*, 10.　　**197.** Cf. Cat., 64. 126 ff.

198. 2185, ff.　　**199.** 351.　　**200.** Vol. I., p. 405.

201. Cat., 68. 57 ff.　　**202.** Cf. Cat., 70. 3-4.

203. Cat., 8.　　**204.** Cat., 99.　　**205.** Cat., 85.

NOTES

206. Mary Augusta Scott, *Elizabethan Translations from the Italian*, Boston, 1916, p. 128.

207. Cat., 62. 39–58.   **208.** Cat., 5.

209. Bk. II. Canto XII. 74.   **210.** Sonnet 17; cf. Cat., 51. 4.

211. Cat., 7. 7.   **212.** *F. Q.*, I. 1. 48.

213. *Virgil's Gnat*, 491.   **214.** Cf. Collins, Chapter I.

215. IV. 2. 45.   **216.** 62. 54; & 61. 102.

217. II. 2. 178.   **218.** IV. 1. 43.

219. II. 1. 9; cf. Cat., 86. 6.   **220.** III. 1. 79; cf. Cat., 3. 11.

221. *Camb. Hist.*, VIII. 2.   **222.** Cat., 62. 62.

223. No. 18.   **224.** Cat., 8.   **225.** Nitchie, p. 126.

226. V. 2.   **227.** LVII.; cf. Cat., 70.

228. Cat., 70 and 72.   **229.** Cat., 61. 78.

230. Cat., 62. 39, ff.   **231.** Cat., 5.

232. 109 and 76.   **233.** Cf. Cat., 8.   **234.** Cat., 70.

235. Cat., 8.2.   **236.** Cat., 45.   **237.** No. 85.

238. *Camb. Hist.*, VII. 8.

239. *Among my Books;* essay on *Lessing.*

240. Cat., 82.   **241.** Cat., 13. 14.

242. Cat., 55. 20 ff.   **243.** Cat., 95. 8.

244. Cat., 101.   **245.** Cat., 64. 256 ff.

246. Cat., 95. 8 and 31. 13.

247. *Par. Lost*, 4. 165; cf. Cat., 64. 273.

248. Cat., 35. 11–15.   **249.** Cat., 44. 11–15.

250. Cat., 69.   **251.** Cat., 92.   **252.** 96. 3–4.

253. V. 127 ff.   **254.** Cf. Cat., 66, *passim.*

255. 171, ff.; cf. Cat., 66. 42 ff.   **256.** p. 171.

257. Cf. Phillips' *Song* with Catullus, 85 also.

258. Cat., 7.   **259.** III. 248.

260. Cf. Sellar, *Rom. Poets of the Republic*, pp. 472–3.

261. Cat., 11. 22 and 62. 40 ff.   **262.** Cat., 22. 21.

263. Cf. Cat., 5.   **264.** Cf. Cat., 8. 3.

265. Cat., 68. 70 ff.

266. *The Romantic Movement in English Poetry*, New York, 1909, p. 16.

267. *Congress of Arts and Sciences, Universal Exposition*, St. Louis, 1904, p. 379.

268. Cf., *e.g.*, *Queen Mab*, VIII. 23–24 with Cat., 64. 270 ff.

269. *Life*, 1. 266.   **270.** *Life*, 1. 342.

271. Cat., 31. 7 ff. **272.** Cf. Cat., 64. 273 ff.

273. Cf. Cat., 68. 52. **274.** Cat., 38.

275. Cat., 85. **276.** Cat., 93. **277.** Cat., 75.

278. Cat., 39. **279.** Cat., 13. **280.** Cat., 45.

281. Cat., 101. **282.** *Life*, Vol. II. p. 400.

283. *Camb. Hist.*, XIII, pp. 49–50.

284. Herbert Paul, *Men and Letters*, New York, 1901, p. 21.

285. Cat., 51. **286.** 243; cf. Cat., 64. 16 – 18.

287. 1335; cf. Cat., 64. 276.

288. 41; cf. Cat., 63. 39–41.

289. *In Memoriam*, XVIII; cf. Cat., 31. 14 and 3. 2.

290. *Poets and their Bibliographies.* Cf. B. Wendell, *The Traditions of European Literature*, New York, 1920, p. 555: "Lesbia's Sparrow so tenderly made undying by Catullus."

291. Cat., 101. **292.** LVII.

293. Memoir, Vol. II, p. 247. **294.** Cat., 31. 13–14.

295. Chislett. **296.** *Appreciations*, p. 258.

297. Taylor, p. 244. **298.** Duff, p. 328.

299. Lionel Johnson, *The Classics*. **300.** p. 81.

301. Duff, p. 322.

BIBLIOGRAPHY

CHISLETT, WILLIAM, JR., *The Classical Influence in English Literature in the Nineteenth Century, and other Essays and Notes.* Boston, 1918.

COLLINS, J. CHURTON, *Studies in Shakespeare.* New York, 1904.

CORNISH, F. W., *The Poems of Gaius Valerius Catullus (Translated by)* in *The Loeb Classical Library.* New York and London, 1919.

CRANSTOUN, JAMES, *The Poems of Valerius Catullus, translated into English Verse, with life, excursus and notes.* Edinburgh, 1867.

DUCKETT, ELEANOR S., "Some English Echoes of Catullus," in *The Classical Weekly.* xv. 177–180 (1922).

DUFF, J. WIGHT, *A Literary History of Rome.* London, 1909.

ELLIS, ROBINSON, *Catullus in the Fourteenth Century.* London, 1905.

ELLIS, ROBINSON, *The Poems and Fragments of Catullus, translated in the metres of the original.* London, 1871.

GAYLEY, CHARLES MILLS, and KURTZ, BENJAMIN PUTNAM, *Methods and Materials of Literary Criticism, Lyric, Epic, and Allied Forms of Poetry.* Boston, 1920.

GOLDMARK, RUTH INGERSOLL, *Studies in the Influence of the Classics on English Literature.* New York, 1918.

LAMB, GEORGE, *The Poems of Caius Valerius Catullus, translated with a preface and notes.* London, 1821.

MACKAIL, J. W., *Latin Literature.* New York, 1903.

MACNAGHTEN, HUGH, *The Story of Catullus.* London, 1899.

MARTIN, SIR THEODORE, *The Poems of Catullus Translated into English Verse, with Introduction and Notes.* Edinburgh and London, 1863.

MUSTARD, WILFRED P., *Classical Echoes in Tennyson.* New York, 1904.

NITCHIE, ELIZABETH, *Vergil and the English Poets.* New York, 1919.

[231]

BIBLIOGRAPHY

Noël, François, *Traduction Complète des Poésies de Catulle*, etc. Paris, 1803.

[Nott, Dr. John,] *The Poems of Caius Valerius Catullus, in English Verse, with the Latin text revised, and classical notes.* London, 1795.

Palmer, Henrietta R., *List of English Editions and Translations of Greek and Latin Classics Printed before 1641.* London, 1911.

Saintsbury, George, *A History of Criticism and Literary Taste in Europe.* New York, Edinburgh and London, 2d Edition, 1902.

Schwabe, Ludwig, *Catulli Veronensis Liber.* Berlin, 1886.

Slater, D. A., *The Poetry of Catullus: a lecture.* Manchester, 1912.

Symonds, John Addington, *Wine, Women and Song: Mediaeval Latin Students' Songs, now first translated into English Verse, with an essay.* New York and London, 1907.

Taylor, Henry Osborn, *The Classical Heritage of the Middle Ages.* New York, 1903.

[Tennyson, Hallam,] *Alfred Lord Tennyson, a Memoir, by his Son.* New York and London, 1897.

Tremenheere, J. H. A., *The Lesbia of Catullus arranged and translated by.* London, 1897.

Ward, A. W., and Waller, A. R., *The Cambridge History of English Literature, edited by.* 14 Vols. New York and London, 1907–1917.

INDEX OF CATULLUS POEM
INDEX OF AUTHORS

INDEX OF CATULLUS POEMS

INDEX OF CATULLUS POEMS

INDEX OF CATULLUS POEMS

INDEX OF AUTHORS

INDEX OF AUTHORS

[239]

INDEX OF AUTHORS

INDEX OF AUTHORS

[241]

INDEX OF AUTHORS

INDEX OF AUTHORS

INDEX OF AUTHORS

INDEX OF AUTHORS

Our Debt to Greece and Rome

AUTHORS AND TITLES

AUTHORS AND TITLES

HOMER. *John A. Scott.*

SAPPHO. *David M. Robinson.*

EURIPIDES. *F. L. Lucas.*

ARISTOPHANES. *Louis E. Lord.*

DEMOSTHENES. *Charles D. Adams.*

THE POETICS OF ARISTOTLE. *Lane Cooper.*

GREEK RHETORIC AND LITERARY CRITICISM. *W. Rhys Roberts.*

LUCIAN. *Francis G. Allinson.*

CICERO AND HIS INFLUENCE. *John C. Rolfe.*

CATULLUS. *Karl P. Harrington.*

LUCRETIUS AND HIS INFLUENCE. *George Depue Hadzsits.*

OVID. *Edward Kennard Rand.*

HORACE. *Grant Showerman.*

VIRGIL. *John William Mackail.*

SENECA THE PHILOSOPHER. *Richard Mott Gummere.*

APULEIUS. *Elizabeth Hazelton Haight.*

MARTIAL. *Paul Nixon.*

PLATONISM. *Alfred Edward Taylor.*

ARISTOTELIANISM. *John L. Stocks.*

STOICISM. *Robert Mark Wenley.*

LANGUAGE AND PHILOLOGY. *Roland G. Kent.*

AUTHORS AND TITLES

AESCHYLUS AND SOPHOCLES. *J. T. Sheppard.*

GREEK RELIGION. *Walter Woodburn Hyde.*

SURVIVALS OF ROMAN RELIGION. *Gordon J. Laing.*

MYTHOLOGY. *Jane Ellen Harrison.*

ANCIENT BELIEFS IN THE IMMORTALITY OF THE SOUL. *Clifford H. Moore.*

STAGE ANTIQUITIES. *James Turney Allen.*

PLAUTUS AND TERENCE. *Gilbert Norwood.*

ROMAN POLITICS. *Frank Frost Abbott.*

PSYCHOLOGY, ANCIENT AND MODERN. *G. S. Brett.*

ANCIENT AND MODERN ROME. *Rodolfo Lanciani.*

WARFARE BY LAND AND SEA. *Eugene S. McCartney.*

THE GREEK FATHERS. *James Marshall Campbell.*

GREEK BIOLOGY AND MEDICINE. *Henry Osborn Taylor.*

MATHEMATICS. *David Eugene Smith.*

LOVE OF NATURE AMONG THE GREEKS AND ROMANS. *H. R. Fairclough.*

ANCIENT WRITING AND ITS INFLUENCE. *B. L. Ullman.*

GREEK ART. *Arthur Fairbanks.*

ARCHITECTURE. *Alfred M. Brooks.*

ENGINEERING. *Alexander P. Gest.*

MODERN TRAITS IN OLD GREEK LIFE. *Charles Burton Gulick.*

ROMAN PRIVATE LIFE. *Walton Brooks McDaniel.*

GREEK AND ROMAN FOLKLORE. *William Reginald Halliday.*

ANCIENT EDUCATION. *J. F. Dobson.*